Let's Talk About Math

Let's Talk About Math

The LittleCounters® Approach to Building Early Math Skills

by

Donna Kotsopoulos, Ph.D.

and

Joanne Lee, Ph.D.

Wilfrid Laurier University
Waterloo, Ontario, Canada

·P A U L·H·
BROOKES
PUBLISHING C°.®

Baltimore • London • Sydney

Paul H. Brookes Publishing Co.
Post Office Box 10624
Baltimore, MD 21285-0624

www.brookespublishing.com

Typeset by Scribe Inc., Philadelphia, Pennsylvania.
Manufactured in the United States of America by
Sheridan Books, Chelsea, Michigan.

Cover image © istockphoto/monkeybusinessimages.

Individuals described in this book are composites or real people whose situations are masked and are based on
the authors' experiences. In all instances, names and identifying details have been changed to protect confidentiality.

Kotsopoulos, D., & Lee, J. (2012), LittleCounters®. United States Trademark and Patent Office: An Agency of the Department of
Commerce, Serial Number: 85392260.

Library of Congress Cataloging-in-Publication Data
Kotsopoulos, Donna, author.
   Let's talk about math : the LittleCounters® approach to building early math skills / by Donna Kotsopoulos, Ph.D., and Joanne Lee, Ph.D.
      pages   cm
   Includes bibliographical references and index.
   ISBN 978-1-59857-589-7 (pbk. : alk. paper) — ISBN 1-59857-589-9 (pbk. : alk. paper) — ISBN 978-1-59857-764-8 (epub e-book) —
ISBN 1-59857-764-6 (epub e-book)
   1. Mathematics—Study and teaching (Early childhood)—Activity programs. 2. Early childhood education—Activity programs.
3. Numeracy—Study and teaching (Early childhood)—Activity programs. 4. Child development. 5. Group guidance in education. I. Lee, Joanne, 1970– author. II. LittleCounters (Program) III. Title.

   QA135.6.K697 2014
   372.7—dc23   2014008095

British Library Cataloguing in Publication data are available from the British Library.

2018   2017   2016   2015   2014

10   9   8   7   6   5   4   3   2   1

Contents

About the Authors

Donna Kotsopoulos, Ph.D., is Associate Professor in the faculty of education and the faculty of science (Department of Mathematics) at Wilfrid Laurier University in Waterloo, Ontario, Canada. She is a former elementary and secondary school mathematics teacher. Dr. Kotsopoulos is a certified member of the Ontario College of Teachers. She is the director of the Mathematical Brains Laboratory, and she is the codeveloper of LittleCounters®, a program aimed at supporting parents, caregivers, early childhood educators, and teachers in developing an understanding of early mathematical cognition. She is also the cofounder and coeditor of the *Fields Mathematics Education Journal*. She is a member of the Canadian Mathematics Educators Study Group. Her interdisciplinary research focuses on mathematical cognition and mathematical teaching and learning across the lifespan, with a current focus on early childhood. Dr. Kotsopoulos has published in many prominent journals and has presented at conferences worldwide.

Joanne Lee, Ph.D., is Associate Professor in the Department of Psychology at Wilfrid Laurier University in Waterloo, Ontario, Canada. She is Director of Laurier Child Language and Math Lab and is a codeveloper of LittleCounters®. Her research focuses on early language and mathematics development using observational and experimental methodologies to conduct both empirical and qualitative studies. One of her aims is to develop effective early childhood education programs and learning strategies to help young children acquire strong mathematical foundations. Dr. Lee has published in leading journals such as *Developmental Psychology and Cognition*. She is currently serving the editorial board of the *International Journal of Behavioral Development*. She is also serving on two editorial boards for introductory psychology university textbooks.

Acknowledgments

Many of our LittleCounters® families and early childhood educators come up to us after our workshop to ask where they can buy a book with the content we have shared with them. They provided the impetus for us to pen this book, with the hope that it may benefit adults who are interested in introducing early numeracy in a fun manner to children. With our sincere gratitude, we wish to take this opportunity to thank the many people and organizations who have made our research program, the LittleCounters workshop, and this book a reality.

This book could not have been possible without the editorial committee at Paul H. Brookes Publishing Co. and the anonymous reviewers, for their faith in our work and in this book. In particular, we would like to thank Astrid Zuckerman and Sarah Zerofsky. Astrid has been instrumental in bringing this book to the publishing world. We thank Astrid and Sarah for their countless hours, expertise, and patience in preparing this book. We would also like to thank Allison Eady for her editorial support and the Office of Research Services at Wilfrid Laurier University for awarding us a book preparation grant.

Our LittleCounters workshop was developed as a result of our findings from our research program. Thus we wish to thank the following funding agencies for supporting our early numeracy research: Canada Foundation for Innovation (CFI); Ontario Research Fund, for supplying Joanne's research equipment; and the Social Sciences and Humanities Research Council (SSHRC). The inception and continuation of our LittleCounters workshop have been supported by many individuals and organizations. We wish to thank Joan Taylor, manager of children's services at Waterloo Public Library, who took a chance with us to introduce our very first LittleCounters workshop at the library in April 2009. No such early numeracy workshop/program for families with children between 1 and 3.5 years old was offered in the region before then. We would like to thank the Fields Institute, University of Toronto, and the Office of Research Services at Wilfrid Laurier University for sharing the same passion about early numeracy by providing us with seed funding to get the workshop running.

Our LittleCounters workshop has always been offered to families in our community in the Waterloo region at no cost. Many organizations have made this possible: the Actuarial Foundation of Canada (2012–2015), Google Canada (2013), and the Kiwanis Club of Elmira (2012–2013). We wish to thank Rob Donelson and Christine McKinlay from the development office at Wilfrid Laurier University for their tireless effort to secure corporate sponsorship so that our LittleCounters workshop can be offered in more venues.

What we have managed to achieve thus far is not ours alone. Our dedicated team of students—undergraduate, graduate, and even high school students completing their educational co-op placement in our labs—have generously contributed their time to make our LittleCounters workshop an enjoyable and enriched experience for the participating families and their young children. Our sincere appreciation goes to our three special graduate students: Samantha (Sam) Makosz, Joanna Zambrzycka, and Anupreet (Anu) Tumber. Sam and Joanna have contributed significantly to the content and delivery of our LittleCounters workshop. Our heartfelt gratitude extends to the families and their children who participated in our early numeracy research project and our LittleCounters workshop. Their participation made this book possible. We also extend our gratitude to many parents, caregivers, early childhood educators, and teachers who have shown such keen interest in our work and in raising LittleCounters.

Last but not least, we send our love and thanks to our family members who supported our efforts through their care, patience, good humor, and enthusiasm. Donna would like to thank Evan Branidis, Ryan Branidis, Fanoula (Fanny) Kotsopoulos, Frieda Rubletz (and family), Helen Chaktsiris (and family), and Colleen Riggin. Joanne would like to thank Eric Terry (her better half of 20 years), Josh Terry, Lee Guan Yong and Lam Sow Chen (her parents), and Robert and Donna Terry (her in-laws).

We are also deeply grateful to our friends who also listened and supported us. Donna would like to thank Carol Beynon, Rebecca Coulter, Teresa Mosher, Boba Samuels, and Cathy Smuk. Joanne would like to thank Hind Al-Abadleh, Joan Meek, Sue-Anne Tu, Susanna Wong, and Eileen Wood.

To Evan and Ryan Branidis
— Donna Kotsopoulos

To Eric and Josh Terry
— Joanne Lee

Introduction

Mathematics is too important to be left to chance, and yet it must also be connected to children's lives.

National Association for the Education of Young Children (NAEYC)
and the National Council of Teachers of Mathematics (NCTM) (2002)

We (Donna and Joanne) have been research collaborators since 2007. I (Donna) am a former elementary school teacher and have primarily focused my academic work on mathematics teaching and learning. Joanne has a deep background in early childhood cognitive development and psycholinguistics. Our research brings together our interdisciplinary expertise in mathematics education and developmental psychology and has largely focused on the ways in which young and school-age children come to know and understand mathematics. We look closely at the role of the environment and the ways in which adults such as parents, caregivers, and early childhood educators (ECEs) can support a young child's mathematical development.

This book is an outgrowth of all our research but was primarily inspired by one of our research projects in which we explored the ways parents, caregivers, and ECEs used mathematical play and language to support the development of counting and other basic mathematics for young children before preschool (Lee, Kotsopoulos, & Tumber, 2010; Lee, Kotsopoulos, Tumber, & Makosz, in press). Preschool children are those children between the ages of 4 and 6 who have yet to start formal schooling. Although some research has been done on the impacts of mathematically rich learning environments on preschool children's mathematical ability and achievement (Clements & Sarama, 2007; National Center for Education Research, 2008; VanDerHeyden, Broussard, & Cooley, 2006), relatively few studies exist that explore the same impacts on younger children between birth and formal schooling. These studies report compelling evidence that suggests that 1) young children are very capable of engaging in more complex ways of understanding counting, numbers, and mathematics and 2) coming to school with a robust understanding of mathematics has very important implications for future learning (Blevins-Knabe & Musun-Miller, 1996; Duncan et al., 2007; Geary, Hoard, Nugent, & Bailey, 2013; La Paro & Pianta, 2000; Romano, Babchishin, Pagani, & Kohen, 2010). Simply put, children who come to school knowing more about numbers and simple mathematics do better in mathematics, and this advantage continues throughout their schooling.

In one of our studies, we had the opportunity to watch more than 200 adult (i.e., parent) and child pairs engaged in play using a preset selection of objects (Lee, Kotsopoulos, & Tumber, 2010).

We presented the pairs with objects such as building blocks, various collections of similar objects (e.g., farm animals, vehicles), and several large foam dice that could elicit numerical activities such as counting, sorting, and classifying. Our initial analysis of the video data we collected revealed that adults in our study actually used very little mathematical talk and engaged in very little mathematical play with their young children between 1 and 3.5 years old. Our results were not totally unexpected, as parents in North America often focus on naming objects (e.g., ball, cup) rather than counting during their daily interactions with their young children. Our findings did cause us some concern.

Children are estimated to receive up to 1,000 hours of literacy education at home and in child care environments before they start formal schooling (Adams, 1990; Cunningham & Allington, 1994). However, for many children from Western cultures, mathematical learning beyond simple sorting, rote counting, and patterning begins only with formal schooling between ages 4 and 6. Not surprisingly, children's mathematical ability and understanding make huge leaps once they begin formal schooling. Some would argue that these leaps happen because children starting school are at a developmentally appropriate age where they are ready to learn number concepts. Others have suggested that the leaps are largely due to schooling or an enriched environment and that mathematical learning could begin much earlier than the start of formal schooling. For example, studies show that children from Asian countries come to school with a greater understanding of counting, numeracy, and other mathematical concepts than children from Western countries such as the United States and Canada (Miller, Kelly, & Zhou, 2005). Adults in Asian countries provide more mathematical opportunities for young children. As a consequence, children from many Asian countries tend to outperform children from most Western countries from the start of schooling, and this trend continues throughout formal education, as can be seen in international standardized testing such as the Programme for International Student Assessment (PISA) by the Organisation for Economic Co-operation and Development (OECD; Mullis, Martin, & Foy, 2008; Organisation for Economic Co-operation and Development, 2012; PISA, 2006).

Given that children could come to school knowing and doing more mathematically, formal schooling is a form of intervention right from the very start. Most children will be catching up on what they could have been doing before the start of schooling, had they been given certain opportunities in their early childhood environments. For young children from disadvantaged backgrounds, the catch-up is more profound than that of their peers and creates a lag that can be insurmountable without focused attention by educators and policy makers (Barbarin et al., 2008; Pappas, Ginsburg, & Jiang, 2003; Pianta, Barnett, Burchinal, & Thornburg, 2009).

Some argue that a societal investment in early childhood education is the solution, rather than playing a game of catch-up at the start of formal schooling. The research supporting this position is undeniable. Children who come to school knowing more do better. However, investment in early childhood education has broader economic implications for society. It is estimated that for every dollar spent on early childhood education prior to formal schooling, there is a return to society of approximately $3 for every child, and this return is well into the double digits for those children from disadvantaged backgrounds (Alexander & Ignjatovic, 2012; Heckman & Masterov, 2004).

Given these findings, we wondered about the impact of enriching mathematical environments for young children and how we could contribute to the advancement of mathematics education for younger children before they start formal schooling. This is where our current research and community outreach are focused. Given what we know from research on young children's brains and their innate mathematical abilities, more mathematics education should be possible in early childhood. Furthermore, as with children from Asian countries, increases in mathematically rich environments should affect not just early mathematics learning but also mathematical competence later in life.

Watching the videos from our study made me (Donna) reflect back 15 or so years on my role in my own children's mathematical learning prior to the start of their formal schooling. At the time, I was not yet an elementary school teacher and had no premonition that understanding mathematical thinking and learning would become the focus of my life's work. I recalled a conversation I had with a kindergarten teacher about ways in which I could help my eldest son, Evan, develop his counting at home. Much to my surprise, Mrs. Scott, Evan's kindergarten teacher, explained to me that, although Evan could recite numbers well into the double digits like a poem, he had difficulty counting a set of objects and recognizing when to stop counting (e.g., when he had counted each object once and only once). He also had difficulty understanding and recognizing how many objects he had just counted. As with most parents, although I had the best of intentions for preparing my child for formal schooling, I did not understand what I could be doing to facilitate mathematical play in ways that would support or enhance my children's mathematical development.

Joanne recalled a similar situation with her son, Josh, who was a toddler at the time. She recalled how her son stopped counting the coasters on their coffee table when he counted to 10. At this point, he paused and looked at her with an expression that said, "Mom, what comes next?" She realized that Josh needed the next series of number words (i.e., from 11 to 20) to keep him going in his counting. To her surprise, Josh was able to count up to 14 successfully when he heard them. It took another week for Josh to successfully count to 20. This incident prompted Joanne to start her research on mathematical input by parents during children's formative years in 2006.

The parents in our study were in exactly the same position we had been in as parents more than a decade ago. If we had known what to do or how to do things differently in terms of mathematical play, we would have done it. We believe most adults would also be building in some mathematical play in their everyday interactions with their children if they knew how to do so effectively. Most of us, as parents, do not know what our young children can do. Our findings in this regard provide the impetus for both this book and our early numeracy workshop called LittleCounters®.

Parents and caregivers are not alone in not knowing how to include mathematics in play and thus focusing more on literacy in early childhood education (Cannon & Ginsburg, 2008). Early mathematical learning is not as significant a focus as literacy development for most ECEs (Barbarin et al., 2008; Cross, Woods, & Schweingruber, 2009; Early et al., 2005; Tudge & Doucet, 2004). Early mathematical learning has also not been a key focus in ECEs' training and education. Consequently, research shows that ECEs are at a disadvantage in terms of knowing how to incorporate mathematically rich play into early care and learning environments (Ginsburg, 2010; Ginsburg et al., 2006).

Other research shows that even elementary school educators often miss spontaneous opportunities to engage children in mathematical thinking, mostly because of their own lack of understanding of mathematics and mathematical concepts (van Oers, 2010). Much of the current literature and practice in early mathematics learning focuses on the start of formal schooling in preschool or kindergarten. However, even after children start school, teachers are often underprepared in their own understanding and comfort levels with mathematics, and parents continue to be unprepared to support their children's learning at home.

Based on our research findings; other research on parents', caregivers', and ECEs' understanding of early mathematical development; and our belief in the need for early childhood mathematics education for parents, caregivers, and ECEs, we developed a community-based early numeracy workshop series called LittleCounters in fall 2008. The workshop series is research based but not exclusively informed by our own research. In fact, the most significant theoretical contributions to LittleCounters come from Gelman and Gallistel (1986), who have identified the key elements of counting for young children.

The aim of LittleCounters (which is described in detail in Chapter 2) was to introduce adults who have young children in their care to ways in which they can develop counting and other mathematical concepts through what we refer to as *purposeful play.* This form of play (also described in detail in Chapter 2) privileges children's choices in play but also requires adult interaction and engagement to support and advance learning. In this workshop series, it is not our intention to push for formal education programs or teaching formal mathematical concepts to very young children. Instead, the goal of LittleCounters is to introduce foundational basic mathematical concepts to young children via daily interactions such as play or snack time.

LittleCounters has been enormously popular and well received by parents and ECEs in Ontario, Canada, where we are based. Our local workshops usually have long lineups of adults with young children in strollers waiting for the limited number of seats in our seminars. We have also received many requests to present this workshop across Canada and internationally. This book outlines the key concepts presented in the workshops: 1) using mathematical talk, 2) engaging in purposeful play to support and advance learning, 3) supporting the development of counting beyond simple rote counting, and 4) providing mathematically rich environments before formal schooling. This book makes accessible the content of the workshops for those that cannot attend in person.

We stress that LittleCounters is not a curriculum. Instead, it is a set of workshops aimed at increasing adults' understanding of children's early mathematical learning and building skills for incorporating early mathematics into daily activities before the start of formal schooling.

This book is intended for *any* individual caring for or raising a LittleCounter. We have attempted to write this book in accessible language for the wide range of adults that are involved in the care and nurturing of young children between the ages of 1 and 5. One does not need to be a mathematician to understand and implement the concepts and ideas of LittleCounters.

Young children are cared for in a variety of settings before they start school. Approximately 60% of young children are cared for in homes by parents or other family members, with the other 40% of children attending structured child care or early learning centers (Barnett, Carolan, Fitzgerald, & Squires, 2012; Coople, 2004). We hope that readers of this book will be adults—parents, grandparents, uncles and aunts, babysitters, ECEs, early childhood policy makers—across these two domains of home *and* structured learning settings. Our sincere hope is that this book can provide the most important facts about early childhood mathematical education in simple language. We believe that preschool mathematical education is not particularly complicated and can be included in children's daily activities without complex recommendations and guidelines. Rather than following a formal curriculum, preschool mathematics education should be closely related to children's play and their own developmental paths.

As the quote from the National Association for the Education of Young Children (NAEYC) and National Council of Teachers of Mathematics (NCTM; 2002) states at the beginning of this introduction, mathematics is too important to be left to chance. The joint position statement from NAEYC and NCTM also reveals another important fundamental belief: Mathematics is too important to be left to formal schooling. As teachers and parents ourselves, our aim was to produce a book that was accessible and contained the appropriate amount of information for parents or ECEs to empower themselves to make a difference in a child's early mathematics learning. Many parents, caregivers, and ECEs have shared their own mathematics phobias with us during our workshops. By showing how easy it is to incorporate counting activities and mathematical talk in daily interactions with young children, we also hope to reduce mathematics phobia for us all.

In this book, we examine the existing research on children's early mathematical learning and the importance of play and play environments. We discuss the importance of counting and activities to develop counting skills through mathematical play and talk. Counting, although important, is not the only mathematics children can and should learn prior to formal schooling. Consequently, we also review other types of mathematical thinking that young children can and should engage in prior to formal schooling. Based on what we know about children's mathematical capabilities and learning, we explore ways to include all these mathematical concepts in children's everyday routines and activities. Finally, we include some important considerations for when your child starts formal schooling.

Where appropriate, we have provided illustrative examples, vignettes, and sample scripts of dialogues between adults and children. Wherever possible, we have drawn from our experiences with families in their homes or from the LittleCounters workshops. All names are fictitious or used with permission. Some concepts are repeated in the book, where appropriate, to emphasize ideas and to facilitate reading.

This book is divided into seven chapters, each focusing on a different aspect of children's early mathematical learning:

- Chapter 1 outlines what research tells us about early mathematical understanding, ability, and development. The chapter shows how young children have more innate mathematical ability than a parent or ECE might initially think.

- In Chapter 2, we explore different types of play and how play environments and activities may be organized or facilitated in ways that can optimize children's mathematical learning.

- Chapter 3 is all about counting. Our main focus in this book is on counting. Meaningful or "rational counting," as some describe it, is different from simple rote counting. This type of counting is proving to be the crucial cognitive skill that underpins children's potential for future mathematical learning. This chapter introduces the five essential counting principles: stable order, one-to-one correspondence, order irrelevance, cardinality, and abstraction. These counting principles, first described by Gallistel and Gelman (1990), have been found to be crucial in supporting mathematical learning and in demonstrating mathematical ability at the onset of schooling. In this chapter, we also introduce our early numeracy workshop series called LittleCounters and describe some of the important and useful play-based strategies that we have found to be effective in the workshops and in our research.

- Chapter 4 brings play and counting together through mathematical talk. In this chapter, we describe the importance of pairing mathematical learning with mathematical talk. The evidence is clear that mathematical talk supports a child's mathematical learning.

- In Chapter 5, we review other types of mathematical thinking that young children can and should engage in prior to formal schooling.

- In Chapter 6, we explore how to include all the mathematical ideas from the previous chapters in everyday routines.

- Finally, in Chapter 7, we include some important things to consider and know about when your child starts formal schooling.

- In Appendix A, we provide some examples of the types of activities we do in LittleCounters. The list is not intended to be exhaustive or complete. It is simply meant to inspire you to come up with your own ideas and activities.

- In Appendix B, we provide a list of counting books that we highly recommend.

- In Appendix C, we list some songs and poems that make use of numbers and/or counting.

We wish you happy counting with your LittleCounters. Know that by reading this book and consciously thinking about the ideas contained here when engaging with a child, you are raising a LittleCounter and undoubtedly making an impact on his or her mathematical learning.

Mathematical Brains of Young Children (Birth to 5 Years)

It might be surprising for you to know that infants can tell the difference between one to three objects just a week after they are born! In fact, very young children can learn about numbers well before they begin school. A simple example of this is showing an infant two bowls with different quantities of cookies an equal distance away and allowing him or her to choose one bowl by crawling to it. Research shows that infants will often choose the bowl with more cookies, suggesting that infants understand the idea of quantity even before they have language for it.

The period between birth and formal schooling is a time of rapid development and is perhaps the most critical and formative period of a person's life. Infants learn to talk with remarkable proficiency just from watching and listening. Children move from being fully dependent on adults for all aspects of their care to being able to eat on their own, dress and groom themselves, and gradually do more and more activities independently. This all happens with remarkable speed! However, although these skills emerge quickly throughout early childhood, it is important to keep in mind that children develop and progress at different rates. As the National Association for the Education of Young Children (NAEYC; 2009) states, "Developing and learning proceed at varying rates from child to child, as well as uneven rates across different areas of a child's individual function" (p. 11).

Infants begin by wanting to explore, and as they gain movement and mobility, they become toddlers who want to be independent and try things for themselves. Most of us have heard a toddler proclaim, "I do!" when faced with a task. Humans, from birth, have an ability to learn and adapt that is unlike any other species. One notable change during early childhood can be seen in the brain structure. Over the first 4 years of life, an infant's brain grows to almost 80% of the size of an adult brain. This fact is remarkable given the time it takes, for example, for the rest of our bodies to mature to adult proportions. Children's brains not only grow rapidly in size but also begin to activate and refine different brain functions. In fact, synaptic activity (firing of neurons) in the brain is strongest before the age of 4 and actually decreases after that point (Huttenlocher, 1984).

Young children also experience rapid changes in their mathematical development. If we were to ask parents and early childhood educators (ECEs) if infants know mathematics, they would probably say "No." Most of us associate the word *mathematics* with algebra or even trigonometry. However, research has shown that infants do understand basic mathematics. In fact, infants as young as 1 week old are able to differentiate among groups with one, two, or three objects (Antell & Keating,

1983; Starkey, 1992; Starkey, Spelke, & Gelman, 1983; 1990). As such, some neuroscientists and cognitive scientists believe that infants are born with some innate abilities to work with numbers (e.g., Carey, 2009; Dehaene, 2011). It would seem that humans come with built-in mechanisms for numbers. Indeed, recent studies measuring infants' brain waves reveal there is a specific area in the right brain (the parietal cortex) that is specifically sensitive to quantities, but not shapes, as early as 3 months old (e.g., Izard, Dehaene-Lambertz, & Dehaene, 2008).

SENSITIVITY TO QUANTITIES/NUMEROSITY

Infants' ability to understand the concepts of more and less is well illustrated in a study by Feigenson, Carey, and Hauser (2002), who presented 10- and 12-month-old infants with the option of "more" or "less" crackers simultaneously. With remarkable consistency, the infants chose the plate with "more" crackers. Many parents use sign language with infants as a preverbal communication system to facilitate their learning. Amazingly, one American Sign Language sign very commonly used by children is "more" (Figure 1.1).

Clearly, there is evidence of preverbal knowledge of numbers in infants. The sensitivity to quantities (i.e., numerosity) seen in 1-week-old infants continues to develop over the 1st year of life (Starkey & Cooper, 1980). For example, 4- to 7½-month-old infants can tell the difference between a set of two objects and a set of three objects but not between a set of four objects and a set of six objects. Six-month-olds are able to discriminate between even larger quantities if the number of objects in one set is twice that of the second set (e.g., six versus twelve objects; Xu & Spelke, 2000). Infants who are 9 months and older can discriminate between a set of four and a set of six objects successfully (Lipton & Spelke, 2003; 2004). At this age, infants show the ability to detect arithmetic changes in the number of sets; for example, they understand that 5 objects added to a set of 5 should sum up to 10 and not 5 (McCrink & Wynn, 2004).

The same sensitivity to quantities that infants can show with objects also applies to sounds; infants as young as 6 months old can tell the difference between 8 and 16 tones but not between 8 and 12 tones (Lipton & Spelke, 2003; 2004). By about 9 months of age, infants can tell the difference between 8 and 12 tones but not 8 and 10 tones. In sum, by around 10 months of age, early numerosity, such as the ability to compare quantities of sets, appears to be in place (Brannon, 2002; Feigenson et al., 2002).

Children learn the basics of language, numbers, self-regulation, and social norms before they start formal schooling. The historical structure of formal schooling depends on some expectations of what young children ought to come to school knowing and doing.

Figure 1.1.   More!

Given the widespread and compelling evidence that children who come to school ready to learn do better throughout their education (Duncan et al., 2007; La Paro & Pianta, 2000), it is important for parents, caregivers, ECEs, and policy makers to understand what young children know and how they learn in the preschool years.

In this book, we refer to many important studies that have contributed to our understanding of what infants and children know and how they learn, along with the implications of these findings for children's academic outcomes. Given that infants cannot talk, how do we know what they know? How do we know what toddlers might know if they do not have a sophisticated communication system in place? The studies we reference use a variety of methods, including observing young children and their parents, caregivers, or ECEs in their daily activities or as they carry out specially designed and developmentally appropriate tasks at home, in an early learning and care setting, or in a lab setting. We also use these methods in our own research.

By around 10 months of age, early numerosity, such as the ability to compare quantities of sets, appears to be in place.

Studies of infants and toddlers are complex, because they do not yet have the full mastery of language needed to tell us what they know and do not know. Infants' and toddlers' motor skills may also depend on their age. As such, two methods are commonly used with children between birth and 30 months old: the *habituation paradigm* and the *intermodal preferential looking method.*

The first method for studying infants and toddlers, the *habituation paradigm,* is most appropriate for infants from birth to 12 months old (Xu & Spelke, 2000). Infants in habituation studies are shown stimuli over and over again until the stimuli become "known" or no longer novel. In essence, habituation happens when the child gets bored of the stimulus. This happens remarkably fast—often within a minute or so—but the time to habituation can vary in different study settings. In these experiments, when the stimuli are changed, the expectation is that children will look longer at the new or different representation of the stimulus than they would if they were shown the initial stimulus, to which they have been habituated. In the case of numerosity studies, an infant is shown one object until habituation is achieved. Then the object is covered and another object is added to it. When the cover is removed, a young child who notices the change in quantity will look longer at the two objects, because he or she only expects one object to be revealed and now there are two. This is known as a *violation of expectations.*

The second method, commonly used with young children between 12 and 30 months old (and which we have been using in our own research), is the *intermodal preferential looking method* (IPL; Hirsh-Pasek & Michnick Golinkoff, 1998; Spelke, 1994). This method relies on observing infants' eye gazes and the way they shift their attention to visual stimuli. During IPL studies, children are seated two feet back from the center of two side-by-side computer monitors, each displaying a different video event. For example, the first screen might show one waving hand, whereas the second shows two waving hands (Figure 1.2). While these videos are being shown, a speaker plays an auditory stimulus spoken in infant-directed speech to accompany the video clip (e.g., a voice saying, "Look! Two hands!"). In these studies, researchers are interested in which of the images the child associates with the spoken stimulus. If infants have learned to associate the word label with the correct visual representation of that quantity, they should look longer at the matching image when they hear the target number word (Lee, Kotsopoulos, Tumber, & Maskoz, forthcoming). In Figure 1.2, the child was asked to look at "two hands."

IPL is an innovative method for studying early mathematical development before children start to produce intelligible speech. It enhances our understanding of the mechanisms involved in early cognitive development when infants are still learning both their native language(s) and numbers. It is well known that children understand language before they can produce it through speech (e.g., Naigles, 2002). This suggests that children might also understand mathematics before they can express their

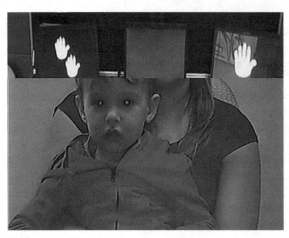

Figure 1.2.   IPL image.

understanding verbally. Indeed, our research using IPL reveals that toddlers as young as 20 months old understand the number word *one* (Lee, Kotsopoulos, Tumber, & Makosz, forthcoming), and some studies using puppets report that toddlers understand *one* at 24 months old (e.g., Wynn, 1990). Using IPL to study infants' understanding of mathematics can help us better understand early cognitive development. We are currently using IPL to study early geometry development by exploring how and when 2-year-old children begin to know typical and atypical rectangles, triangles, circles, and squares (Kotsopoulos & Lee, forthcoming).

Once a child has a fairly developed communication system in place, other research methods may be more suitable. For example, puppets can be used to study their knowledge and thinking processes. Puppets are commonly used with children who are 2 years and older and seem to establish a more comfortable and play-like setting for them. This method was used in a respected study by Karen Wynn (1992b) to understand how and when children know number words.

Throughout this book, we reference the important research that has contributed to the current understanding of how children develop mathematically, what innate resources they come with, and how we, as adults, can support them in their learning of mathematics through-out early childhood and into formal schooling. In the interest of making our book easily accessible, precise details of the experiments are not included. Rather, we invite interested readers to explore the references at the end of the book for publications with more details of the research we cite.

LINKING NUMEROSITY TO NUMBER WORDS

With the acquisition of language, infants begin the road to linking their early understanding of numerosity to knowledge of number words such as *one* and *two* (e.g., Huttenlocher, Jordan, & Levine, 1994; Jeong & Levine, 2005). Language is an important means for all of us to represent and organize our number knowledge to, for example, count and ultimately do advanced mathematics. Without language, we would not be able to count very efficiently, as shown in a study on the Piraha tribe in the Amazonia region of Brazil, who have a "one-two-many" counting system (Gordon, 2004). In this study, the members in the tribe failed to count past three, as their language does not have number words representing specific higher quantities (Gordon, 2004).

Likewise, by 5 or 6 years old, kindergartners can only accurately count the number of objects that matches the number words they understand (LeFevre et al., 2006). This ability to count objects, beyond the detection of more or less by infants before they develop language, depends on the child's education in a language or communication system that matches words to quantities.

By the age of 2, most toddlers can say their first number words, but they do not have a complete understanding of what these words truly mean (Sarnecka & Carey, 2008; Wynn, 1990; 1992b). Between the ages of 2 and 3, children begin to know that number words are quantity words (Gelman & Gallistel, 1986) that are different from adjectives such as *big* or *red* (Geary, 2006). In previous studies using the puppet method (Wynn, 1990; 1992b), toddlers have been shown to understand the meaning of *one* (e.g., Gelman, 1993; Wynn, 1990; 1992b) around 2.5 years old, to know the meaning of *two* by 3.0–3.5 years old, and to understand *three* by 3.5– 4.0 years old. Using the IPL method, we found that toddlers as young as 20 months old know the meaning of *one* (Lee, Kotsopoulos, Tumber, & Maskoz, forthcoming). In sum, by 2.5 years old, children know that *three* objects are more than *two* objects, perhaps by using visual cues, but they may still be unable to associate the number word *three* with a group of three objects. An example of the difference between knowing word numbers and understanding counting came up in one of our workshops, as discussed in Text Box 1.1.

COUNTING

When do young children know their 1, 2, 3s? It happens around 3 years old. You might immediately think, "I know a child or children younger than three that know 1, 2, 3!" In this book, when we refer to counting, we are referring to an ability more complex than just rote counting (i.e., being able to recite the numbers). Knowing about the meaning of numbers and reciting numbers are very different. Our intention so far has been to show how children are able to count before they begin formal schooling. In this section, we discuss the different types of counting (beyond just rote counting) that include verbal, object, and mental counting.

Counting with meaning is a critical developmental milestone for children and sets the foundation needed for all other mathematics (Baroody & Wilkins, 1999; Fuson, 1988; Lee et al., forthcoming). In our LittleCounters® workshop, we focus on object counting, because young children need visual aids to help them associate meaning with number words as they count. During each of our LittleCounters workshop sessions, a variety of objects for counting, such as bean bags with both number symbols and nonsymbolic representations of numbers (e.g., two dots to represent the number two; Figure 1.3), sandbox number shapes, and muffin tins with numbers written inside, are provided to each parent–child pair.

We also aim to provide some suggested toys that parents, caregivers, and ECEs can use to incorporate counting in their daily interactions. Any object in a child's environment can be counted, but we have found the objects mentioned previously to be particularly helpful

---

||||||| TEXT BOX 1.1.   MY 2-YEAR-OLD CAN COUNT TO 12!

When Cassandra and her son Ryan attended LittleCounters® for the first time, Cassandra proclaimed that Ryan could count to at least 12 or 13. Our first activity that day involved a poem about frogs on a log: "Five frogs sitting on log. One frog. Two frogs. Three frogs. Four frogs. Five frogs. Five frogs all fall off the log." During this activity, parents were asked to count the five frogs with their child and then put one frog at a time on their arm (as the log) while they recited the poem, culminating with the frogs falling off their arm. Ryan counted the frogs. He missed one and Cassandra corrected him. Halfway through the poem, with three frogs left on the imaginary log, Ryan was asked if there were more frogs on or not on the log. Ryan pointed to the log. After the frogs fell, Cassandra asked him to count the frogs with her to make sure they had all the frogs in the imaginary pond. He missed counting one of the frogs and when asked about how many frogs he counted, he started tossing the frogs.

Nonsymbolic   Symbolic

Figure 1.3. Nonsymbolic and symbolic.

for children learning to recognize both symbolic and nonsymbolic representations of number words (Figure 1.4).

When toddlers and preschoolers count from the number one into the double digits, they often skip one or more numbers and will sometimes say numbers in the wrong order. For example, a young child may count, "One, two, three, five, six, seven, nine, eight, ten!" In this example, the number four is missing and the numbers eight and nine are out of order. These sorts of counting errors are not uncommon when young children are first learning about numbers and counting.

It has been suggested that children start by learning *verbal counting* (Clements & Sarama, 2009, p. 21). As one study put it, children start counting "by starting at the beginning and saying a string of words, but they do not even 'hear' counting words as separate words" (Clements & Sarama, 2009, p. 21). The number words children recite may not even be in order, because they do not understand the meaning of the order of these words or that the order even matters! This type of counting is often referred to as *rote counting* (Baroody & Wilkins, 1999). Rote counting is similar to reciting a poem—children can recite a series of words, but the number words might not carry any meaning or they might not connect them to the context in which they are counting (Fuson, 1988). This type of counting often starts before age 2.

In contrast to rote counting, verbal counting is counting that involves an association of numerical meaning with the words being spoken and the order in which they are used. In verbal counting, *one* represents one object; *two* represents two of something and follows after the number one. Similarly, *three* represents three of something and follows after the number two and so forth. Clements and Sarama (2009) propose that verbal counting does not involve objects but instead represents an understanding of the stable order of the number words; it is the root of quantitative thinking (p. 21). In contrast, *object counting* is the ability to link the words used in verbal counting with quantities of objects in ways that allow us to answer the question, "How many?"

Text Box 1.2 illustrates the importance of the difference between rote counting and "real" counting. Young children start learning numbers via rote counting, and rote counting helps them remember the names of numbers. However, we must be mindful of the difference between rote

Rote counting is similar to reciting a poem—children can recite a series of words, but the number words might not carry any meaning or they might not connect them to the context in which they are counting.

Verbal counting is counting that involves an association of numerical meaning with the words being spoken and the order in which they are used. In verbal counting, *one* represents one object; *two* represents two of something and follows after the number one.

Object counting is the ability to link the words used in verbal counting with quantities of objects in ways that allow us to answer the question, "How many?"

| | | | | | | **TEXT BOX 1.2.   ROTE COUNTING ISN'T "REAL" COUNTING!**

Michelle and her 26-month-old daughter, Emma, are playing make-believe farm with many cow, pig, and chicken toys at home. Emma lines up six cows to get ready to go into the barn and starts counting:

Emma: 1 cow, 2, 3, 4, 5, 6, 7, 8, 9, 10. Mommy, I have 10 cows!

Michelle: Let's see. We have 1 cow, 2 cows, 3 cows . . . 6 in total. How many cows are going into the barn, Emma?

Emma: No, I have 10 cows because I counted to 10.

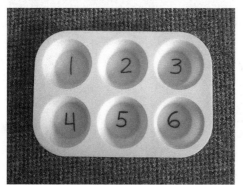

Figure 1.4.   LittleCounters® toys.

counting and real counting, which requires the understanding of one-to-one correspondence between a number word and an object in a set as well as the total quantity in a set. A one-to-one correspondence refers to an object in a set being counted once and only once.

Building on Clements and Sarama's (2009) work, we propose that early verbal counting may also include objects. Toddlers try to link the few number words they know to the objects in a set but perhaps are not able to do so accurately. For example, toddlers about 20 months old have been observed to count repeatedly "one, two, one, two" when shown a set of four objects. To demonstrate knowledge of counting, the child must be able to count the objects without using a counting word for an object more than once. Two objects cannot both be *one* in the count sequence. This is called *one-to-one correspondence*. In Figure 1.5, when a child is counting the 4 objects and saying, "one, two, one, two," the child may not know or be able to apply the correct counting words and thus repeatedly count objects with the same number word. Even preschoolers regularly violate the counting principle of one-to-one correspondence by skipping over objects or recounting objects previously counted.

It is only around 30 months that most children are able to count without repeating objects (Sophian, 1988; Wagner & Walters, 1982). Therefore, the developmental progress of counting may start with rote counting (before age 2) and then move from early verbal counting (with objects) to verbal counting before reaching object counting. By age 5, children routinely engage in *mental counting* that may or may not involve any objects and is done without words (e.g., "mental" mathematics for which the calculations are done in one's head).

Even after 5 years of age, children or even adults may still use objects to facilitate counting, but this should not be taken as an indication of an inability to count. Sometimes counting with objects is necessary to understand a given quantity. For

"One,   two.   One,   two."

Figure 1.5. Counting example.

example, an ECE counting the number of young children waiting in line to go outside for outdoor play will likely have to do a count of each child (i.e., object).

To learn verbal counting of objects in a set, toddlers and preschoolers must first learn the sequence of the number words, the meanings of all the number words in their counting range, as well as the *cardinality principle* (e.g., Gelman & Gallistel, 1986). The cardinality principle refers to the fact that the last number in verbal counting sequences—for example, the word *three* used in counting "one, two, three"—represents the total number of items in the count (i.e., three items). In addition to understanding the cardinality principle, toddlers must also understand the concept of *ordinality*—the idea that higher numbers refer to more items and lower numbers refer to fewer items in an array (Bisanz, Sherman, Rasmussen, & Ho, 2005). Children who do not understand that the last number counted represents the total number in the set will not be able to answer the question "How many?" when counting objects or even be able to tell you their age. For example, when counting to three, a child might give the number four when asked how many objects she has counted in the set.

Around 4 years of age, children start to master the counting system based on the concepts of cardinality and ordinality, and by age 5 or 6, they can use it to find out the number of objects in a set (Wynn, 1990; 1992b). By 5, most children are able to count up to 10 objects and indicate correctly that the last number counted is the total quantity in the set (Baroody & Wilkins, 1999; Freeman, Antonucci, & Lewis, 2000; Fuson, 1988).

Counting into the double digits requires even more skills and understanding. Although most young children can rote count into the double digits by the time they start school, an understanding of numbers beyond nine requires learning some additional concepts. These concepts include 1) the way in which decades of numbers shift at the number nine (e.g., 9, 10; 19, 20); 2) the names of higher numbers (e.g., 13, 20, 30); 3) rules for generating decades of numbers (e.g., decade plus single digits—21, 31, 41); and 4) exceptions to the rules (e.g., the way the teens are named; Baroody & Wilkins, 1999).

Most 4-year-olds can also count objects in a set backward from 10 to 1 (Clements & Sarama, 2009, p. 36). Counting backward is often seen in counting books and in children's songs and poems about numbers. We discourage counting backward until children are able to demonstrate the counting principles we introduce in this chapter. In Chapter 3, we discuss these "counting principles" more fully and their implications for mathematics learning.

The cardinality principle refers to the fact that the last number in verbal counting sequences—for example, the word *three* used in counting "one, two, three"—represents the total number of items in the count (i.e., three items).

The concept of *ordinality* refers to the idea that higher numbers refer to more items and lower numbers refer to fewer items in an array.

SUBITIZING

Consider the small set of mailboxes in Figure 1.6. How many mailboxes are there?

Did you have to count them? Or did you know just by looking that there were four mailboxes? This ability to know how many there are in a set without counting is called *subitizing*. Subitizing refers to the ability to spontaneously recognize the total quantity in a set without verbally counting the objects.

Some scientists view subitizing as a form of rapid subconscious counting (e.g., Gelman & Gallistel, 1986). Scientists also suggest that subitizing may actually emerge before counting and paves the path for learning the counting system (e.g., Le Corre, Van de Walle, Brannon, & Carey, 2006). Toddlers as young as 2 years old can recognize the quantities of one and two without counting (Mix, Sandhofer, & Baroody, 2005). Typically, children begin to recognize one, then two, then three, and then four (Le Corre et al., 2006). By kindergarten, most children can recognize and name the total quantity of up to four objects in a set without counting.

> *Subitizing* refers to the ability to spontaneously recognize the total quantity in a set without verbally counting the objects.

Around 5 years old, children can mentally work with the numbers of objects in separate sets to come up with the total quantity without actually counting the objects. For example, they can tell you that two groups of two and one group of three make up a total of seven objects, without having to count each of the objects. Scientists do not yet agree on whether subitizing is a prerequisite skill for counting or if it is an ability that develops as children learn to count, but it is widely accepted that subitizing is closely related to the development of counting and arithmetic skills (Hannula & Lehtinen, 2005).

ORDINALITY, ORDERING NUMBERS, AND ORDINAL NUMBERS

Ordinality refers to the relationships between numbers, with some numbers representing more and some representing less (Miller, Kelly, & Zhou, 2005). To understand ordinality and to answer questions such as "Which is bigger, three or two?" correctly, children have to understand two key principles of ordering numbers. They need to know that 1) a set of three objects is a collection of two plus one more (Zorzi, Priftis, & Umiltà, 2002) and 2) each successive number in a number sequence (e.g., one, two, three) represents a set that has more in quantity than the number before it (e.g., three is more than two, and two is more than one; Griffin, Case, & Siegler, 1994).

> *Ordinality* refers to the relationships between numbers, with some numbers representing more and some representing less.

In developing an understanding of ordering numbers and ordinality, toddlers begin first by constructing *hierarchical inclusion*—the idea that one is included in two, two is included in three, and so forth. Therefore, adults should focus on very small numbers with toddlers. They can do this easily through play—for example, by saying and showing, "Look, I have one pig. Here comes another one walking over. Now I have one, two—*two* pigs!"

Figure 1.6. Mailboxes.

Preschoolers around the age of 3 begin to show an understanding of number order (which number comes first) in comparing sets of numbers between one and three, and this understanding has been found to be independent of their counting skills (Huntley-Fenner & Cannon, 2000; Mix, Huttenlocher, & Levine, 2002). By the age of 4 or 5, children can tell which of the two numbers is bigger with sets of numbers larger than four (e.g., four versus six; Siegler & Robinson, 1982).

Hierarchical inclusion is the idea that one is included in two, two is included in three, and so forth.

Tasks that compare sets of objects in terms of which are bigger and smaller are known as *magnitude comparison tasks*, where *magnitude* describes the "manyness" or quantity of the set of objects (Noël, Rousselle, & Christophe, 2005). As outlined previously, very young children start by learning to tell the difference between very small sets of objects in very specific ratios. However, they do not yet understand that the higher the number in the counting sequence, the more "manyness" that number represents in comparison to the previous numbers. Because they do not understand the association between number words and "manyness," preschoolers tend to do better on nonsymbolic comparisons of magnitude versus symbolic (Mazzocco, Feigenson, & Halberda, 2011; Nosworthy, 2013).

Both children and adults have an easier time distinguishing between sets that have a wider numerical span between them (Dehaene, Bossini, & Giraux, 1993). For example, when comparing two pairs of numbers—four versus five and four versus nine—the second comparison would be easier. The more numerical distance between the two numbers, the easier the comparison (Figure 1.7).

Tasks that compare sets of objects in terms of which are bigger and smaller are known as *magnitude comparison tasks,* where *magnitude* describes the "manyness" or quantity of the set of objects.

Humans seem to organize numbers mentally from smaller to larger and from left to right, and this may be related to the way we learn to read (Dehaene et al., 1993; Fias & Fischer, 2005). However, some languages are read in different directions (e.g., Arabic is read from right to left), so cultural differences do appear in children from cultures in which reading is not left to right (Fias & Fischer, 2005).

The joint position statement on early childhood mathematics from the National Association for the Education of Young Children (NAEYC) and the National Council of Teachers of Mathematics (NCTM; 2002) emphasizes the need for educators to understand cultural diversity so that they are able to meet the learning needs of all children, regardless of their social, ethnic, or linguistic variations. Evidence suggests that cultural differences can have an impact on children's learning, and these differences raise important considerations for teaching and learning (Brooker, 2010; Miller, Major, Shu, & Zhang, 2000; K.F. Miller et al., 2005). For example, cultural differences have been misunderstood as cognitive

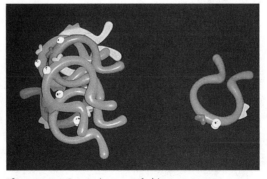

Figure 1.7. Comparing sets of objects.

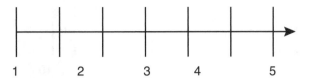

Figure 1.8. Number line.

impairments for some minority and disadvantaged children, highlighting the need for educators to understand the ways in which culture might shape a child's learning (Gutiérrez, Bay-Williams, & Kanold, 2008; Robinson, 2010; Torres-Velasquez & Lobo, 2004).

It is thought that children develop a mental number line as they learn to order numbers. This number line is a representation of the arrangement (and relative magnitude) of numbers in ascending order on a line in our minds (Zorzi et al., 2002). A visual representation of the number line can be seen in Figure 1.8. This visual representation is not actually the way the image looks in one's mind, but rather this is a visual illustration of the cognitive concept of the mental number line.

There has been some debate on how the mental number line is understood by young children as they develop an understanding of numbers. Some suggest that numbers are more incrementally and equally spaced (Gallistel & Gelman, 1992). Others propose that as numbers become larger, they are more compressed and clustered as seen in Figure 1.9 (Dehaene, 1992).

Regardless, there appears to be some sort of mental number line structure that organizes numbers and their numerical relationships to one another. To tap into this mapping of numbers in research, children are asked to look at a number line with a beginning and an end point (Siegler & Opfer, 2003). The end point can be 10 or higher. They are then asked to indicate where, for example, the number three or the number seven would be on the number line.

The ability to use the visual representations of the mental number line begins with formal schooling (around 6 years old) and a complete and accurate representation of numbers on the mental number line is only achieved by Grade 6 (Siegler & Opfer, 2003). The mental number line is strongly related to the ability to add and subtract (Siegler & Booth, 2005) and to the ability to find the relative position and magnitude of numbers (Siegler & Booth, 2005).

Besides knowing that numbers can be ordered in a sequence, young children also learn that numbers arranged in line or in sequence assume different names in English. The number-one object in a sequence is not called *one* but instead called *first* (Figure 1.10). Words such as *first*, *second*, and *third* are referred to as *ordinal numbers*.

Words such as *first, second,* and *third* are referred to as *ordinal numbers.*

A study conducted in the United States that asked preschoolers to pick out ordinal objects in a sequence found that 72% of preschoolers could pick out the first object and 13% of preschoolers could pick out the third object in the line (Sarama & Clements, 2009). Around 5 years of age, children can identify and use ordinal numbers from *first* to *tenth*. We will discuss ordinal numbers in more depth in Chapter 5. Our point here is that young children not only come to know numbers and counting words but also learn the meanings of various counting words.

ARITHMETIC

The term *arithmetic* refers to the manipulation of numbers, including addition, subtraction, multiplication, and division. Infants as young as 9 months old have shown the ability to add (5 + 5) and subtract (10 – 5; McCrink & Wynn, 2004). As we discussed earlier, 2-year-olds show an understanding that quantity changes when you add or remove one or two objects in a set (Starkey, 1992). This understanding of quantity change is not as precise as the ability children ultimately develop,

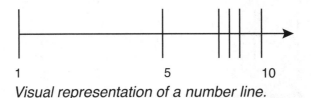

Visual representation of a number line.

Figure 1.9. Compressed number line.

which includes the ability to perform arithmetic operations using counting strategies and mental mathematics. Younger children understand that quantities can be more or less but might not yet understand how much a sequence of objects increases or decreases. By the time they are 4 years old, most children know the exact quantity change in tasks that require adding or removing up to four objects (Huttenlocher et al., 1994). Subitizing, the automatic subconscious assessment of quantity we discussed earlier, is likely the mechanism that makes this sort of rapid knowledge of quantity change possible.

Preschoolers and kindergartners have been observed using a variety of counting strategies to help them in calculation tasks such as addition and subtraction. These strategies include verbal counting (e.g., saying, "There are six objects here and two objects there. If we bring them over, then there are seven, eight—that makes eight for six plus two"), counting fingers, counting up from the larger or smaller number, and fact retrieval (i.e., recalling from memory facts already known; e.g., Siegler & Jenkins, 1989). Until the time they reach the age of 6, most children still rely on the use of physical objects to perform adding or subtracting operations with a larger number of objects between five and eight (Huttenlocher et al., 1994).

CHAPTER SUMMARY

This chapter provides a glimpse of what young brains are capable of learning in early mathematics. Remarkably, young children can do much more than we might think and certainly much more than is currently expected of them prior to formal schooling. Infants as early as 1 week old appear to have an intuitive sense of numerosities and quantities. This early sense of numerosity enables young children to master foundational mathematical concepts such as counting before they start formal schooling. Children who can count with ease by the time they reach kindergarten have been shown to achieve arithmetic and overall mathematics competence in years to come (Penner-Wilger et al., 2009). Thus counting is a cornerstone of early numeracy competence and should be a focal point for education in the preschool years (NCTM, 2000).

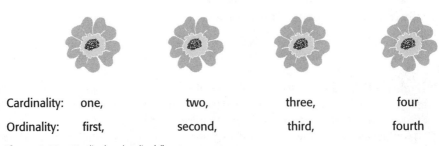

Cardinality:	one,	two,	three,	four
Ordinality:	first,	second,	third,	fourth

Figure 1.10. Cardinal and ordinal flowers.

2

Purposeful Play

<hr>

Consider the following example as a guiding scenario: In your backyard, local park, school yard, or classroom, there is a sandbox. Children can use a variety of objects in the sandbox during play. Sometimes children use toys such as cars and trucks in the sandbox. On other occasions, children use rocks and sticks to draw in the sand and build structures. Other times, children bring containers to fill with sand to build structures such as sandcastles. Finally, children sometimes just play in the sand with their hands and their feet. How can mathematical learning be promoted in the sandbox?

<hr>

Play is the most significant learning activity that young children engage in during early childhood (National Association for the Education of Young Children [NAEYC], 2009; The Canadian Association for Young Children [CAYC], 2001). In some sense, every play environment is also a learning environment (Hirsh-Pasek, Michnick Golinkoff, Berk, & Singer, 2009). Even routine daily tasks can be learning opportunities and can be made to feel like play. Take, for example, going up or down stairs with a child. You can count each step, sing a counting song, or change the tone of your voice to emphasize a concept and increase a child's interest. The child may then think of walking up the stairs as a game or other form of play, which can help him or her learn early mathematical concepts such as counting and numbers.

All children learn implicitly and explicitly from their interactions with objects and with people (Johansson, 2004). Adults can play an important and critical role in supporting and guiding a child's play toward mathematical thinking. Even the most unexpected objects can be used to mathematize play by using everyday objects in counting games that support mathematical learning. *How does this happen?* This chapter explores how a play toy can become a learning toy that can be used to teach a mathematical concept and how parents, caregivers, and early childhood educators (ECEs) can evaluate how much children have learned and what further learning can or should happen.

The environment shapes both *what* an individual learns and the *how* an individual learns (Piaget, 1962; 1976/1929). Some studies have shown that children who experience environments rich in mathematical talk and activities in early childhood have advantages in mathematical learning and skills when starting formal school (Klibanoff, Levine, Huttenlocher, Vasilyeva, & Hedges, 2006). For learning to occur in a play environment, the play must be relevant and engaging to the child and must also be developmentally appropriate (NAEYC, 2009).

The term *developmentally appropriate* refers to typical age ranges or phases in learning progression in which milestones are usually evident in young children. Sometimes, "developmentally appropriate" activities are associated with a child's age, but this may not always be the case. Children learn different knowledge and skills at different paces. For example, some children show increased understanding of the concept of "how many" right after they turn 3 years old, whereas other children learn this concept later in their 3rd year or after they turn 4. Asking an 18-month-old "How many?" and expecting an answer might be premature. It may be developmentally inappropriate because it is outside the typical age range when this level of understanding is known to emerge. This does not mean that we cannot or should not still ask such questions. Instead, we can ask young children mathematical questions without expecting correct or consistent answers. The challenge for adults is to know when developmentally appropriate milestones are possible. In other words, many parents, caregivers, and ECEs do not know the age ranges in which children can start to learn different types of mathematics. The purpose of this book is to help parents, caregivers, and ECEs better understand when and how young children can learn mathematics.

Studies show that the quality of mathematical play is also important (Park, Chae, & Foulks Boyd, 2008). Evidence suggests that high-quality mathematical play in early childhood is correlated to mathematics achievement levels well into the middle school years. For example, LeFevre and colleagues (2009) describe how the children of families who engage in activities that have a counting component, such as board and card games, have higher later achievement in mathematics after the start of schooling. Similar results are seen in the area of block play. Children whose parents build complex block constructions with them show higher mathematics achievement 1 year later (Lee, Kotsopoulos, & Zambrzycka, 2013). So when we talk about quality of play, we are talking about three things: 1) opportunities for interactions between children and adults, 2) activities that have mathematical components, and 3) the intent to highlight mathematics through these play interactions.

It is important to be mindful that there are cultural differences in the types of play children might engage in and in the value given to play in different cultures (Brooker, 2010; NAEYC, 2009). Although it is clear from cross-cultural studies that all children engage in some form of play, there are differences in the ways that they play (Brooker, 2010; Hirsh-Pasek et al., 2009). Sometimes these differences in play have a philosophical or economic basis. Getting to play every day and focusing on play as a context for life and learning are typical in Western cultures but not so typical in other cultures. Children from countries or backgrounds with greater economic hardships are often expected to contribute to the work of the family, and these children often differ in both their approach to play and the frequency with which they get to play (Brooker, 2010). Although play is universal, the way in which play happens, the frequency of play, and the type of play children engage in and are accustomed to vary from child to child.

Given the importance of play in early childhood, and given what we have outlined in Chapter 1 about young children's abilities to understand numbers and simple mathematical concepts from birth, it would seem both reasonable and wise to think about ways to incorporate mathematical learning in play. As we will discuss in the next section, this is, in fact, fairly easy to do.

MATHEMATICS MADE PLAYFUL AND MATHEMATIZING ELEMENTS OF PLAY

Researcher Bert van Oers from the Free University of Amsterdam in the Netherlands (1996) was among the first to make the important distinction between making *mathematics playful* and making *play mathematical.*

In *mathematics made playful*, mathematics learning is the primary goal, and the elements of mathematical knowledge are transformed into some kind of play activity. Take, for example, the musical numbers game we use in our LittleCounters workshop (Text Box 2.1).

According to Cross and colleagues (2009), games with mathematics as the primary focus, rather than the supplementary focus, are more effective in advancing learning of mathematics for young children (p. 2). Thus the idea of mathematics made playful is important for providing an enriched learning environment for children.

The mathematics made playful approach puts the mathematics first in organizing play for a child. This is not to say that all play should be organized around mathematics. However, only approximately 6% of time in early learning settings such as preschools is focused on mathematics (Early et al., 2005). There is a clear need for expanding a mathematical focus in educational play.

TEXT BOX 2.1.   MUSICAL NUMBERS

Have you ever played musical chairs? In musical chairs, people go around a group of chairs until the music stops. As soon as the music stops, everyone must quickly sit on a chair. The number of chairs is usually one fewer than the total number of people playing. During our LittleCounters® session, we play musical numbers, which is similar to musical chairs. We use foam mats with numbers on them, scattered throughout a room. When the music stops, children quickly jump onto a mat. They then identify the number and count to that number using their fingers, to the best of their ability. Our version of the game continues for the duration of the song without any children being eliminated or until the children's attention shifts. Children can usually focus on this game for the length of one song. The purpose of this game is to learn about the symbolic representations of numbers and practice counting. Musical numbers is one of many ways that mathematics is made playful during LittleCounters.

Things on the home front are equally unpromising. One 2004 study reported that 90% of parents of preschool and kindergarten children believe that schools are primarily responsible for children's mathematical development (Evans, Fox, Cremaso, & McKinnon, 2004). On the other hand, only 43% of the same sample of parents reported that the school is responsible for literacy development.

We can see from these findings that not much time is spent on mathematical activity in most home, child care, and early learning settings. This might be because it is assumed that learning mathematics happens after formal schooling. However, many parents, caregivers, and ECEs report having a general anxiety toward and even dislike of mathematics, which might further reduce their likelihood of emphasizing mathematical play in the preschool years (Cross, Woods, & Schweingruber, 2009, p. 8).

Another way to develop early mathematics skills involves *mathematizing elements of play activities*. In mathematizing play, the child's play is emphasized and the parent, caregiver, or early childhood educator tries to introduce elements of mathematics into the child's existing play activities. This can be done by taking up the child's spontaneous mathematical or mathematics-like actions (such as counting, comparing, relating, and measuring) or by actively eliciting new mathematics-like actions and trying to improve them (van Oers, 1996, p. 5). For example, a child may be included in the daily mealtime routine by having him or her set the table. While setting the table, the child could be encouraged to count utensils, place settings, and objects in order to incorporate mathematics into familiar activities. Another example of mathematizing play can be seen in Text Box 2.2.

 TEXT BOX 2.2.   CAN YOU MAKE IT LONGER?

Three-year-old Xiou is playing with his train set. The set is made of connecting pieces of wood that can be shaped into many configurations to form a railway. Xiou loves to play with his train set! His mother sees him building his train set and comes over and says, "Xiou, your setup of the railway tracks today looks longer than the way you set it up yesterday! How long is it? Let's count the pieces."

Xiou and his mother count the pieces.

His mother then asks, "Can you make it even longer?"

Xiou takes two connected pieces apart and proceeds to add another two pieces.

His mother than asks, "How long is it now?" or "How many pieces do we have to add to make it this long?"

The example in Text Box 2.2 shows how a child's self-initiated play with a train set can become an opportunity for learning about measurement with nonstandard units (see Chapter 5). Xiou's mother also had the opportunity to hear him count and see if he understood the concept of *longer.* Here, we see that Xiou's mother took a play moment and made it mathematical.

Based on his study of 4- to 7-year-olds, van Oers (1996) proposed that opportunities for learning mathematics, such as the one Xiou's mother facilitated, can emerge spontaneously during play. This is different from taking a mathematical concept, such as measurement, and developing a game, riddle, or task that can be used to teach the concept through play. Instead, making play mathematical involves spontaneously mathematizing everyday elements of children's play so that mathematical concepts can be explored in their natural environment.

This approach to mathematizing elements of play is also very different from what some educators might call *direct instruction.* Direct instruction typically involves adults initiating and organizing a lesson around a mathematics topic and is similar to classroom teaching. In contrast, mathematizing elements of play still allows the child to initiate and direct the activity, while the adult fits mathematical content and ideas around his or her play (Cross et al., 2009, p. 225). In mathematized play, a child's play evokes mathematical ideas that can be infused into play; this is very different from a planned activity organized by the adult for the child. In mathematizing elements of play, the adult is not stopping the play and "teaching" in the formal sense of what most people understand teaching to be. Rather, through discussion during play interactions, adults follow the lead of the child, allowing for opportunities for mathematical learning to emerge naturally. To introduce mathematics into a child's play, consider asking the following questions:

- Can you make it longer?

- Can you make it shorter?

- How wide is it?

- How many did you use?

- How do you know if it is strong enough?

- How long did it take you to do that?

- What if we added one more?

- Tell me about your pattern.

Whereas van Oers's conceptualization of play is aimed at teachers, the same important ideas can be used by parents, caregivers, and ECEs of young children.

The task of mathematization may not be easy initially, because parents, caregivers, and ECEs may not have extensive knowledge of mathematics, mathematical cognition, and developmental trajectories. The aim of this book is to introduce the key concepts of mathematics education and help parents, caregivers, and ECEs learn to develop their own strategies for teaching mathematics. The book is also useful for kindergarten teachers looking to understand early mathematical cognition more fully.

In mathematizing play, it is important to consider the developmental appropriateness of different games and skills. The guidelines from the joint statement by the National Association for the Education of Young Children (NAEYC) and the National Council of Teachers of Mathematics (NCTM; 2002) also stress the importance of developmentally appropriate learning opportunities. For example, adding two-digit numbers (e.g., 10 + 12) is likely outside the range of ability for a 3-year-old. However, adding quantities up to five may be more reasonable (e.g., 1 + 2) once the child understands the principles of counting (e.g., one-to-one correspondence, the cardinality principle, the concept of ordinality). For a detailed description of counting principles, see Chapter 3.

For most of us, mathematics involves both quantitative and spatial reasoning. This includes seeing patterns and understanding the mathematical relationship among ideas, concepts, and different mental and physical representations. Later in the book, we discuss counting and other mathematics that should be considered when attempting to mathematize routine elements of everyday play. In this chapter, we focus on the different types of play, the implications of different types of play for learning, and how each type of play may relate to other forms of play when it comes to learning specifically about mathematics. Across all forms of play, the objects with which children engage may be toys, educational toys, or everyday objects.

ADULTS' ROLE IN PLAY

Some suggest that play *belongs to the player;* in other words, play should be initiated by the child and guided solely by the child's interests (Piaget, 1962; Sutton-Smith, 1997). Indeed, children have been known to have their own definition of *play* that is often very different from their definition of *work* (Howard, 2010). Adults play a crucial role in shaping the play environment and guiding learning opportunities emerging from play in ways that support the learning of the child (Fisher, Hirsh-Pasek, Golinkoff, & Glick Gryfe, 2008; Hirsh-Pasek et al., 2009; Howard, 2010). For example, play guided by an adult that involves focusing a child's attention on certain aspects of the play, on problem solving, and/or on inhibiting irrelevant information may improve mathematics and reading (Uren, 2008).

Researchers Ingrid Pramling Samuelsson, Eva Johansson, and colleagues from the University of Gothenburg (Pramling Samuelsson & Asplund Carlsson, 2008; Pramling Samuelsson & Johansson, 2009) suggest that it is not uncommon for children to invite adults to join in play. According to Samuelsson and Johansson (2009), children invite adults to join in play for a variety of reasons; they may require assistance, want to show what they know, or want to find out more information. In Figure 2.1, the father can be seen providing assistance to the child by offering the child another block.

Adults are thought to have three main roles in play: planning for play, supporting play, and reviewing play (National Council for Curriculum and Assessment, 2009, p. 56). Across each of these roles, play provides a good avenue for assessment that can serve as the basis from which planning, supporting, and reviewing emerge. We will discuss assessment and adults' roles in assessment later on in this chapter.

In the next section, we outline three different types of play: free play, play-based learning, and purposeful play. We advocate strongly for purposeful play as way to support and advance a young child's learning. There are many different types of play (e.g., pretend play, guided play, symbolic play) outlined by researchers. Our goal is not to describe all the different types of play but rather, from our perspective, to describe the three categories of play that are most relevant to the main purpose of the book: supporting young children's early mathematical development.

FREE PLAY

Free play is unstructured, chosen, and initiated by the child and engaged in either independently or with a peer or an adult (Hirsh-Pasek et al., 2009). Free play with an adult can involve either 1) coplay, in which the child directs the activities and the role of the adult during play (Johnson, Christie, & Yawkey, 1987), or 2) parallel play, in which the adult is playing beside the child or in the vicinity of the child but not with the child directly (Johnson et al., 1987). Free play does not necessarily lead to learning; sometimes free play may be just play without any added educational value (Ruff & Lawson, 1990).

Free play can also lead to learning and often does, but it is important to remember that learning is not the explicit intent of free play. Instead, learning during free play is incidental. Children are unlikely, for example, to learn about how the geometric properties of a square are different from

Figure 2.1.   Father and child playing.

those of a triangle unless there is some engagement with an adult or peer that draws their attention to certain properties over others.

Many studies point to the ways that free play helps children learn how to structure their own time without depending on an adult to plan for them and learn about the world around them. Free play also helps children exercise autonomy over their time and choices, fosters creativity and imagination, and helps with interpersonal relationships (Dietze & Kashin, 2012; Duncan & Lockwood, 2008; Hirsh-Pasek et al., 2009; Howard, 2010; Ruff & Lawson, 1990; Whitebread, 2010).

Free play may provide good learning opportunities, but because free play is not explicitly focused on learning, learning outcomes are more difficult to see. It is not uncommon for adults to express surprise when a child knows something that is unexpected. Often this unexpected knowledge or skill comes from free play. Learning is wonderfully serendipitous during free play.

Hirsh-Pasek and colleagues (2009) explored the spatial language used by parents in free play with their young children. As our own research and other studies have shown, the use of mathematical language is related to the mathematical achievement of young children (Gunderson & Levine, 2011; Klibanoff et al., 2006; Lee, Kotsopoulos, Tumber, & Dittmer, 2009). Hirsh-Pasek found that parents used relatively little mathematical language during free play and that free play did not inspire the kind of mathematical talk known to be beneficial for subsequent mathematical learning and achievement.

To return to the scenario outlined at the beginning of the chapter, drawing objects in the sand with a stick, driving a toy truck through a sand tunnel, building castles in the sand, or sharing a shovel with a friend are all tasks that might happen spontaneously during free play in a sandbox. Although these activities are not explicitly mathematized play, free play still gives children opportunities to learn other skills such as imagination and socialization with peers.

PLAY-BASED LEARNING

Play-based learning is play that is grounded in implicit cognitive, social, emotional, or physical learning objectives. It is a form of play in which learning is built in through thoughtful and intentional planning by an adult (Dietze & Kashin, 2012). The adult, rather than the child, is the ultimate architect of the play, even though the child has a say in which play he or she engages in. Unlike free play, learning is not serendipitous but rather is an expectation of the activity.

Play-based learning may be child or adult initiated and can involve the child, peers, and/or the adult. When learning becomes an intentional goal of play, such as in play-based learning, an adult becomes an indispensable component of play because he or she determines, plans, and implements the initial play environment.

Adults or even other peers may, in fact, be essential components of play-based learning, because some children may require interactions with others in order to achieve the play's learning objectives (Pramling Samuelsson & Johansson, 2009). Learning objectives in play-based learning are embedded in the context of play, and learning is a hidden outcome of interacting with the learning objects. However, this learning cannot be guaranteed without some form of observation by or interaction with the adult, and it is often difficult for parents, caregivers, or ECEs to set specific learning goals and expected outcomes for play-based learning when they have not learned about mathematics education themselves (Cross et al., 2009, p. 2).

Play-based learning may involve or likely be related to a formal curriculum either mandated through a regional jurisdiction (e.g., ministries of education or government agencies responsible for early childhood education) or adopted independently in early learning settings. Objects that children interact with during play-based learning may be seen as typical toys but are generally chosen by teachers and adults because they are understood to have some educational benefits. The play options available to the children in these settings have been planned and designed with the intention of supporting learning.

In an average early childhood classroom, most ECEs could identify various learning goals associated with "centers" located throughout classroom. This is not to say that children always take up the intended learning goals of these classroom centers. Unless some level of assessment of understanding and knowledge development takes place, there is really no clear-cut way to know for sure if children are meeting the intended learning goals. An example of this can be seen in Text Box 2.3.

In Text Box 2.3, although the task itself was about measurement and counting, Freida was unable to achieve the intended goals. It could be that the range of counting was too high to be

---

 **TEXT BOX 2.3.   HOW MANY APPLES TALL ARE YOU?**

Ms. Rubletz sets up a "center" in her preschool class where children can measure their height using pictures of apples. The main learning goals of the task are to engage measuring using nonstandard units and counting up to 10. The apples are taped onto a chalkboard wall (Figure 2.2). Children come to the center and stand beside the apples and indicate their height with some chalk and write their name. Throughout the day, Ms. Rubletz calls students over to the apples to ask them to show their height in apples. She calls 3-year-old Freida over and asks her about her height, saying, "How tall are you in apples, Freida?" Freida stands beside the apples and says with confidence, "This tall," pointing to the ninth apple. Ms. Rubletz asks Freida to count the apples. Freida starts counting the apples from the bottom of the wall but does not stop at nine. She also misses the number eight. When asked how many apples tall she is, she again points to the ninth apple despite having just counted past the ninth apple to the end of the length of apples.

developmentally appropriate for Freida. Freida did not meet the intended learning goals for the task, and this would not have been evident to the ECE if she had not engaged in conversation with the child. The child's accurate marking of her height against the row of apples shows a partial understanding of the task components but not the overall intended goals.

The scenario outlined at the beginning of the chapter, playing in a sandbox (or sand table or water table), is fairly common in an early learning or care setting. Learning in these settings can be intentionally structured around measurement tools, objects, and instruments. Children have the opportunity to perhaps learn about mathematical concepts such as capacity, volume, or counting through such centers. For example, there may be various shapes of containers that hold the same volume of sand available in the sandbox. Children can be encouraged to pour the sand from one container to another to see if the different-size containers all hold the same amount of sand. Whether the child comes to understand the relationships between the volumes by playing in the sandbox is not fully known, and observing the child is likely not enough to really assess his or her learning.

Similarly, when adults purchase and provide "educational toys" or "educational technology" for children, there is an expectation that interaction with the object or technology will have an educational outcome for the children. In fact, a 2005 study reported that 78% of parents perceive electronic toys/devices as educational (Consumer Electronics Association, 2007). However, educational toys and educational technology should be approached with caution.

Over the past decade, there has been an explosion of toys and technology proposed to be educational. More and more electronic toys are being targeted at infants and toddlers, with sales of electronic toys and devices for children between birth and 15 years old estimated at US$2 billion per year (Consumer Electronics Association, 2007). Those caring for and educating young children are motivated to provide the best possible opportunities for learning and are very willing consumers.

A recent study by Rideout (2011) found that 12% of children between 2 and 4 years old played with technology such as computers, tablets, and electronic games, and 24% of children played with technology at least once a week. However, this use of technology does not necessarily mean children are learning. Our own research and other studies show that the interaction between adults and children using technology facilitates learning better than the technology itself (Cross et al., 2009, p. 253; Lee, Kotsopoulos, Makosz, Tumber, & Zambrzycka, 2013).

Many electronic devices, such as laptops or tablet computers, are explicitly geared toward educational content in early language, literacy, and numeracy and are marketed as having educational value. But what exactly does it mean when some object or piece of technology intended for a child is labeled *educational*? The simple answer is that this label frequently does not mean anything at all. There is often little evidence that products marketed as educational have implications for learning. Although some toy and technology developers conduct research to test the learning outcomes of using their products, the extent to which this occurs is unknown. Most jurisdictions do not place restrictions on toy producers regarding promises of learning associated with toys and technology geared toward children. Products such as the many mobile device applications devoted to early arithmetic may have the potential for facilitating learning. However, in the

Figure 2.2.   Counting apples.

absence of rigorous testing with children, these educational claims are no more than speculative. As we explain in the next section, some intention by the adult to assess the child's learning from an educational toy or technology is essential for facilitating learning.

Interesting research by Seo and Ginsburg (2004) shows that play by preschoolers in an early education setting is already remarkably mathematical. Seo and Ginsburg's study of 90 four- and five-year-olds showed that 88% of young children engage in at least one mathematical activity during 15-minute playtime observations. In their study, the socioeconomic status and gender of the child were unrelated to the amount of mathematical play they engaged in while being observed. The types of mathematical play that were observed involved the concepts of pattern and shape (21%), magnitude (e.g., comparison of two or more items to evaluate relative magnitude; 13%), enumeration (e.g., numerical judgment or quantification; 12%), dynamics (e.g., exploration of processes of change or transformation; 5%), spatial relations (e.g., exploration of positions, directions, and distances in space; 4%), and classification (e.g., systematic arrangement in groups according to established criteria; 2%; pp. 93–96). Overall, their study shows that a considerable amount of mathematical play can happen in a play-based learning setting. This set of findings would seem to contradict an earlier study by Early and colleagues (2005) that reported that only 6% of a child's time is spent on mathematics in an early care or learning center. It may be that children engage in mathematical thinking routinely, without explicit intention and despite the fact that overall programming within the learning setting tends to focus very little on mathematical learning.

As the joint statement by the NAEYC and the NCTM (2002) states, "early childhood . . . needs to go beyond sporadic, hit-or-miss mathematics" (p. 9). The NAEYC and the NCTM are referring to the fact that early mathematical education requires adults to shift to a different type of play with a different intent, thinking about children's emergent learning (which we describe in the next section). In short, even mathematical play does not guarantee mathematical learning and understanding in and of itself. Moreover, mathematical play may go unnoticed by adults if they are not intentionally looking for it.

PURPOSEFUL PLAY

During play-based learning, children engage with learning environments or objects that have been intentionally chosen to stimulate learning. However, the extent to which learning actually happens and the type of learning that has occurred usually are not known and may be quite different from what might have been intended (Pramling, 1983).

Purposeful play combines both free play and play-based learning. In this type of play, a child's learning is assessed through interplay between the child and the adult or between the child and a learning object that has a built-in feedback component (Kotsopoulos & Lee, 2013; Figure 2.3). It is a form of play that both recognizes the child's ownership of play and involves the adult in important ways to support learning (Wood, 2010). We define purposeful play "as the intentional and spontaneous engagement of talk or actions by the adult with the child with the implicit intent of facilitating learning" (Kotsopoulos & Lee, 2013, p. 56). In this book, we focus on purposeful play to promote early mathematics learning. As illustrated in Figure 2.3, purposeful play includes opportunities whereby mathematics is made playful by perhaps intentional selection of educational toys for the child but has at its core the adult's intentional mathematization of play and the use of mathematical talk.

During purposeful play, the child is seemingly engaging in free play or play-based learning. What sets purposeful play apart from the other two types of play is that an adult is intentionally and periodically taking actions, such as starting conversations with the child or even just observing, to assess, further develop, or enhance the cognitive, social, physical, or emotional development of the child. This active engagement by the adult does not take away the self-regulatory control of the play from the child but rather is an outgrowth of the play (Kotsopoulos & Lee, 2013). Purposeful play can also be facilitated through digital learning objects that have a mechanism for providing feedback that allows children to refine or advance their thinking. In this book, we will be focusing on purposeful play that involves adults contributing to play and providing feedback during play.

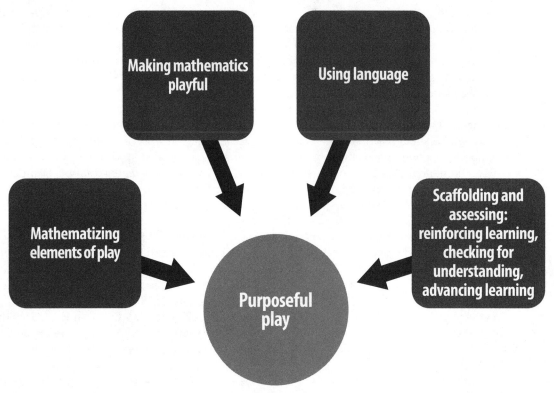

Figure 2.3.   What is purposeful play?

As shown in Text Box 2.4, Ryan's granny's spontaneous engagement with him while he is playing a game of his choice is a good example of how purposeful play can happen. Ryan's granny notices that he misses objects when counting. Making a clear distinction between those objects he has counted and those he still needs to count helps improves his accuracy. The next chapter will talk about the kind of counting Ryan's granny helps him learn when she engages him in this quick counting task. We also discuss specific counting strategies that may be helpful.

Early mathematical learning involves purposeful interactions with an adult or sometimes even a peer that revolve around learning objects. These objects can be counting games, songs, dominos,

---

| | | | | | | | TEXT BOX 2.4.   PURPOSEFUL PLAY

Ryan is 2½ years old and loves pretending he is a farmer and playing with his farm set. It is his favorite thing to do. The farm set he has consists of a barn, fencing to make a corral, a feeding trough, and a large collection of farm animals—some that came with the farm set and some that Ryan has collected. On this particular afternoon, Ryan is lining up his animals to take turns to eat at the trough. He's lined up most of his animals—approximately five. His granny wanders over and says, "Gee Ryan, that's a lot of animals lined up to eat. How many are there?" Ryan points at the animals and proceeds to count, missing one of the animals as he counts. Granny asks him if he's sure that there are four. She suggests that they count them together and move the animals into the corral after they have had their drink. Ryan recounts the animals, moving them over the corral after their drink. This time he counts five. Granny praises him and lifts up her hand to show five fingers! She then goes back to her reading, and Ryan continues playing.

building blocks, and so forth that are related to mathematics. When children play with building blocks, for example, there are many opportunities to engage them in learning about mathematical concepts such as quantity, size, and dimensions. Through purposeful play, adults can take advantage of learning opportunities that emerge naturally out of children's everyday play to mathematize play and build mathematics skills.

Purposeful play should be introduced carefully by adults in ways that support the child's learning but do not intrude totally on the child's playtime and the benefits associated with it (Emilson, 2007; Emilson & Folkesson, 2006). For example, an adult might suggest that the child count objects during play. The child may ignore the adult or object outright. Following the child's lead when he or she indicates a lack of interest in that moment is important. Although young children do involve adults in their play from time to time and for specific purposes, studies have shown that children prefer to play on their own or with other children most of the time (Siraj-Blatchford & Manni, 2008). In addition, most adults simply are not available 24/7 to engage in play with their kids and cannot be expected to turn every game into a teaching moment.

Assessing learning during play is directly linked to purposeful play. However, before we discuss assessing learning through purposeful play, it is important to stress again that free play and play-based learning are also both important and beneficial to children's learning. Purposeful play should not interfere with or even dominate other types of play. Purposeful play can occur intentionally in a play-based learning setting in which free play might also occur. Purposeful play could also be happening through free play in a home setting.

ASSESSING LEARNING THROUGH PLAY

Through our research, we identified three *development-enhancing features* of play that parents, caregivers, and ECEs engage in during purposeful play with their young children: checking for understanding, reinforcing learning, and advancing learning (Kotsopoulos & Lee, 2013). Development-enhancing features are actions adults can take during purposeful play that are useful in supporting and advancing a child's learning.

The first feature, *checking for understanding,* often involves asking questions ("Are you sure?") or presenting the same task in a similar context to see if the child really understands. For example, imagine an adult who hears a child counting incorrectly. The adult can either 1) ask the child if he or she is certain about the counting and ask the child to try counting again or 2) suggest that the child count another, similar set of toys or objects. The second feature, *reinforcing learning,* is closely tied to positive reinforcement (e.g., saying "Great job!") and affirmation ("Yes, you got it right!") of the child's knowledge. The third feature, *advancing learning,* moves a child farther along his or her own learning pathway. It can involve asking challenging questions or proposing tasks aimed at engaging the child in a deeper level of thinking about the mathematical concepts. For example, when a child clearly shows an understanding of counting objects from one to five, a parent could try to engage the child in tasks that involve understanding "How many are in a set?" More examples of how to implement these features of purposeful play can be seen in Text Box 2.5.

By using the three development-enhancing features in purposeful play, adults can understand what a child currently knows and how to promote age-appropriate learning. According to Russian psychologist Lev Vygotsky (1962, 1978), a child's learning pathway can be described as a *zone of proximal development* (ZPD). This ZPD is a hypothetical range that includes a child's current knowledge or understanding of a particular topic, where the child's knowledge and understanding could progress as a result of learning and maturation. Adults can come up with age-appropriate questions and additional play-based tasks that allow the child to move forward in his or her own ZPD. Sometimes a more proficient peer or an older child can also support a child's learning and development.

It is important to note that children can also move themselves along their individual ZPD. There is some evidence to suggest that some learning does happen spontaneously and independently without direct adult input (e.g., Gunderson & Levine, 2011; Vygotsky, 1962). This sort of learning

TEXT BOX 2.5.   FERRYBOATS AND CARS

An 18-month-old toddler is playing with his toy ferryboat that holds cars in the bottom for transporting them across a lake. There are three toy cars that fit in the bottom of the ferryboat. A small ramp unfolds at the bottom of the ferryboat for the cars to be driven into the bottom. The child is counting as the adult and child move two of the cars into the ferryboat. What could parents, caregivers, and ECEs do and say to engage in purposeful play in this scenario?

Checking for understanding	Reinforcing learning	Advancing learning
"How many cars did you count? Can we do that again?"	"That's great counting. Good job getting two cars into the ferryboat!"	"There's one more car over here to go in! How many cars are there now?"
[Child pulls out the cars from the ferryboat and recounts.]	[Child is observed counting the two cars as he moves them into the ferryboat.]	[Child grabs the last car and puts all three into the ferryboat while counting along with the adult.]

might happen during free play or play-based learning. For example, we discussed earlier how, without formal instruction, children develop an understanding of magnitude—the idea of more and less. Children can also understand, without formal or explicit instruction, ordinal relationships such as the "first this, then that" rule, although in limited ways. Some learning theorists, such as Vygotsky, suggest that in general there is only so far along a ZPD that a child can get on his or her own. An adult or more expert other (i.e., another child) is needed at some point to increase a child's progress along his or her developmental pathway.

The development-enhancing features of checking for understanding and reinforcing learning can help establish where on their own unique ZPD children are located. These often occur naturally and are perhaps used unconsciously by adults interacting with children. These two development-enhancing features of purposeful play are in line with the idea of *formative assessment*, which is intended to provide information about a child's prior and emergent learning (Cross et al., 2009, p. 255).

Cross and colleagues (2009) propose that there are three main types of formative assessment that adults engage in: observation, tasks, and flexible interviews (pp. 256–264). Observation is perhaps the most effective way that parents, caregivers, and ECEs can assess children. Observation involves systematically watching and listening to children during play (Cross et al., 2009; Dietze & Kashin, 2012; NAEYC, 2009). Task assessments involve examining the outputs of a child's activities, such as drawings, block constructions, and patterns.

The flexible interview is the approach to finding out what a child knows and does not know that is most aligned with the theory of purposeful play. Flexible interviews involve simply talking with the child. Talking to children can provide some surprising and unanticipated insights into what they know and what they are thinking. At the same time, these conversations can also reveal that the child knows less than we would assume based on observation (Cross et al., 2009, p. 263).

Engaging with children to learn about their own learning and understanding can be challenging. It requires the adult to be able to relate to the child's play, link the play back to learning objectives, and connect a child's current thinking to more advanced, developmentally appropriate ideas. There may only be short intervals of play interaction between an adult and child, which makes the context and the content of these interactions very important (Siraj-Blatchford, Sylva, Muttoch, Gilden, & Bell, 2002).

Another factor that makes understanding children's learning more complicated is that learning is not necessarily linear. As parents, caregivers, and ECEs, we tend to agree with the saying that development is often "one step forward and two steps back." What children might demonstrate one day may be quite different from what they can do on another day. Consistently demonstrating an understanding over a period of time is the hallmark of learning. Random bursts of knowledge or insight that are not consistent over time are not signs of movement along a child's ZPD, but rather they demonstrate hopping back and forth between full and partial understanding. Checking for understanding, a development-enhancing feature of play, is particularly useful in recognizing whether consistent learning over time is evident.

Adults need to be thoughtful about and respectful of a child's play. The play should belong to the player—that is, it should be the child who is in charge (Piaget, 1962; Sutton-Smith, 1997). The contamination of play with adult intention is a concern among many theorists (Piaget, 1962; Sutton-Smith, 1997) and may pose a risk to either play-based learning or purposeful play.

Most adults have experienced a child's reaction when an adult tries to take over his or her play. Children often become disinterested in play or express frustration when an adult intervenes too much. Although purposeful play involves intentional and direct interactions with children to 1) check for the child's emergent understanding, 2) reinforce learning, or 3) advance learning, all these must be done without taking away the child's ownership of his or her play. In short, purposeful play requires parents, caregivers, and ECEs to take advantage of unexpected, but timely opportunities to engage a child in learning about numbers, but this should not translate into turning play into structured learning at all times. This requires adults to pay attention to children's cues as to when and how they want to play and what they are ready to learn. Whitehead (2010) describes this as acting upon play cues to promote cognitive challenges, which then furthers learning. Although the focus of this book is mathematical learning, the development-enhancing features we identified can also be applied to other areas of learning through play.

CHAPTER SUMMARY

As children grow older, play often becomes separate from learning. It is an unfortunate reality that, in some countries, play is viewed as a less effective way to learn compared to direct instruction by adults. Research has consistently shown that play is how children learn about themselves, others, and their world in their early lives. In this chapter, we suggested that some forms of play are more conducive to shedding light on what a child knows and the extent to which learning has occurred. Although learning can happen during free play involving objects or simply imagination, due to the nature of free play, it does not necessary give us much insight on the extent to which learning is occurring.

Play-based learning involves learning as an intentional goal of play, although this might not be obvious to the child. However, again, play-based learning may or may not help children move farther along in their ZPD, and children's progress through this learning is not often measured.

In this chapter, we suggest that purposeful play is a form of play that involves an adult actively engaging in ongoing assessment of the child's current position in his or her ZPD. By assessing a child's current understandings, the play can be transformed by using diverse objects, having discussions, and acting in a way that promotes more learning while checking for the child's understanding. Purposeful play is intended to guide learning in a playful manner. However, the interactions that are part of purposeful play also have many interpersonal benefits, associated with shared fun time together during play.

Adults should exercise caution in engaging in play and respect a child's ownership of play. Play belongs to the child and should not be contaminated with too many extra activities or overstructured by the intentions and goals of adults. A delicate balance is required between playing for pure fun and playing to learn.

Counting with Your LittleCounters

Ask your child to count as high as he or she can. Next, take a small set of objects (one or two for each year of your child's age). Ask your child to count the objects. After your child counts the objects, ask, "So how many were there?" Ask your child to start counting the objects from a different starting point. Ask your child to show you how many objects he or she counted with his or her fingers. Did your child double count any of the objects? If your child counts the objects easily, increase the number of objects and repeat these steps. What does this tell you about your child's counting ability?

The ability to count and understand numbers underpins all other mathematical learning. By the time they go to school at age 4, many children can count well into the double digits. This form of counting may not, however, represent an understanding of numbers necessary for the further learning of mathematics. Sometimes parents and educators unknowingly assume that a child *can* count due to *rote counting*. Although the child might be able to rote count—that is, to recite the numbers from memory—he or she might not have the necessary understanding of numbers to assign meaning to his or her counting. Dietze and Kashin (2012) call counting that involves an understanding of the meaning of the numbers *rational counting* (p. 259).

As we discussed in Chapter 1, there are many different types of counting. Children first learn rote counting, in which the number words have no real numerical meaning to them (Baroody & Wilkins, 1999; Fuson, 1988; Wynn, 1992b). Even before they learn rote counting, evidence suggests that young children are capable of subitizing (rapidly assessing quantity without actually counting; Penner-Wilger et al., 2007). When young children begin to engage in verbal counting, they often use objects in their counting, which helps them connect number words with the numerical ideas they represent (e.g., the word *one* means one object or "oneness").

By about age 3, verbal counting (with or without objects) is fairly stable. Children may continue to use objects for counting, with fingers being the most common and arguably the most important counting tool. Finally, children become very capable of counting mentally (counting in their heads without speaking or using fingers) by about age 4. By this age, children are capable of having a good understanding of what it means to count.

Generally, if children know the number word, then they should be able to demonstrate rational understanding of counting by the time they start school (Dietze & Kashin, 2012). However, this is not always the case. A child may be able to rote count out loud up to 20 or 30, but when given a small set of 3 or 4 objects to count, he or she may count an object more than once. The child may be unable to build a set of objects of a specific number when asked or even count correctly up to 5 objects. For example, he or she may count to a different number when recounting objects in the same set, if asked to use a different object as a starting point, or he or she may not be able to say at the end of counting how many objects were actually counted.

Some children might not experience environments that support their learning of rational counting. Other children might be in environments in which their rote counting is misunderstood as rational counting. Of course, some children just develop numerical understanding at different rates than others (National Association for the Education of Young Children [NAEYC] and National Council of Teachers of Mathematics [NCTM], 2002). Adults need to be mindful of the differences that different environments inspire and the possibility of overestimating a child's abilities because of a false illusion of competency. To help identify evidence of rational counting in children, we utilize the *five counting principles*.

Gelman and Gallistel (1986; Gallistel & Gelman, 1990) were among the first to identify five essential counting principles that are seen in young children who are competent in counting. Adults can use these counting principles to understand a child's comprehension of numbers. These counting principles are *one-to-one correspondence*, *stable order*, *cardinality*, *abstraction*, and *order irrelevance*. It is thought that children develop an understanding of certain principles—one-to-one correspondence, stable order, and order irrelevance—between the ages of 2 and 4 (LeFevre et al., 2006; Wynn, 1990; 1992a). These counting principles have been found to be crucial in laying the foundation for other mathematics learning (Geary, Hoard, Nugent, & Bailey, 2013; La Paro & Pianta, 2000; Sasanguie, De Smedt, Defever, & Reynvoet, 2012).

The first principle, the *one-to-one correspondence* principle, is the idea that, when counting a set of objects, only one number word must be assigned to each item (see Figure 3.1). So when children count with an understanding of one-to-one correspondence, they only assign a single number to any one object in the set, and there is no repeat or double counting of any objects. The object that was counted as one, for example, cannot be counted again as any other number.

The second principle, *stable order*, is the understanding that numbers are used in a fixed order. This principle states that numbers assigned in a counting set are assigned in the same order as in any other set, just like the alphabet. One always precedes two, two always precedes three, and so forth. When children have not yet developed an understanding of this principle, they may have their own stable order list of counting words that differs from the accepted order (Gelman & Gallistel, 1986), as seen in Text Box 3.1.

The third principle is the *cardinality* principle, which states that the number assigned to the last item in the counting set represents the total number of objects of the entire set. If a child is counting a set of three objects and is asked, "So how many did you count?" then the child should be able to say "three" in response if he or she understand the cardinality principle. However, the correct response of the number three is not full evidence of an understanding of the cardinality principle,

One-to-one correspondence

| One | two | three | four | One | two | two | four |

Correct: One count word for each object

Incorrect: Two stars counted twice with the word "two"

Figure 3.1. One-to-one correspondence.

TEXT BOX 3.1.   STABLE ORDER

Stable order

- "One, two, three, four, five, six, seven, eight, nine, ten."

Unstable order

- "One, two, three, five, four, six, seven, eight, nine, ten." (Counting words are out of order.)
- "One, two, three, five, six, seven, eight, nine, ten." (Counting words are missing.)

as the child must also understand the relationship between numbers—that is, three, for example, is more than two but less than four (Fuson, 1988; Wynn, 1992b).

Wynn (1992b) suggests that evidence of understanding of the cardinality principle has two components. First, the child must know the cardinal word meaning (i.e., three means three items) and respond correctly with the last word of the counting sequence when asked "how many?" Second, the child must be able to give the correct number of objects responding to the cardinality of the set and not just the last object counted. For example, when a child has counted a set of three objects and is asked, "Can you give me three?" he or she should give three objects rather than the third object in the set. For numbers larger than three, it is not the case that the cardinal word *four* has to be learned first followed by the cardinality principle. Rather, the learning process is intertwined and simultaneous rather than sequential—as is the case with the numbers one, two, and three.

With quantities fewer than four, children rarely use counting as a strategy to answer the question, "How many?" However, as children get older, they recognize that counting helps answer questions of how many objects are in a set (Fuson, 1988; Wynn, 1990, 1992b). Using counting as a tool for figuring out how many objects are in a set is a strategy that is more typically used by children who have an understanding of numbers up to 10, which tends to emerge around age 4 or 5.

Children who do not understand the cardinality principle will often say an unrelated number when asked, "How many?" For example, if a child is counting a set of three objects and is asked how

 TEXT BOX 3.2.   CARDINALITY

A child is asked to count some mini soccer balls.

"One, two, three, four."
The adult asks the child, "So how many did you count"?
The child says, "Four!"
The adult then asks, "Can you give me four?"
The child grabs two and hands them to the adult. The adult says, "That's not four!"
The child scurries away to another toy.

many, if the child does not understand cardinality, he or she may give a random number—say, *two* or *eight* or any other number.

The dialogue in Text Box 3.2 shows a child who seems to have an understanding of the one-to-one correspondence principle. The child can also give the cardinal word, as we can see from his response of "*four.*" However, when asked to give four, the child picks up two objects. It may be that he does not fully understand "fourness" or that he was simply bored with this interaction. This example illustrates two key points in assessing a child's understanding of counting principles: 1) children should be able to do this sort of counting consistently for you to be sure they understand the counting principles, and 2) they need to be able to both say the last number and give the number of objects when asked in order to demonstrate that they understand the cardinality principle.

We have also observed that when asked "How many?" young children often give their age as the response. Typically, children first understand the one-to-one principle by the age of 2 or 3 and then learn the cardinality principle as they connect the count words to objects in a set within their counting range (Wynn, 1990; 1992b). It is important to note that young children may be able to identify pictures or sets of one or two objects, when asked to point to such representations, before they have a complete understanding of the cardinality principle (Wynn, 1992b), as evidenced through habituation studies of week-old infants (Antell & Keating, 1983; Starkey, 1992; Starkey, Spelke, & Gelman, 1983; 1990). The time between a young child showing evidence of understanding the number *one* and understanding that numbers represent sets of objects or numerosities and a child beginning to show an understanding of the cardinality principle can be about a year, although this may vary from child to child (Wynn, 1992b).

The last two principles, the *abstraction* principle and the *order-irrelevance* principle, describe how the counting process functions. The abstraction principle states that the first three principles—one-to-one, stable order, and cardinality—are applicable to any set of items. Essentially, it involves an understanding that everything and anything is countable! The *order-irrelevance* principle is the understanding that the order in which objects are counted is irrelevant. You can begin counting at any object in the set and still end up with the same number.

In Text Box 3.3, an exchange between a child and an adult shows that the child understands that where the counting begins does not change the total count. Changing the order of the counting of objects in a set is an important strategy and helps children come to know order irrelevance. Note that the order-irrelevance principle also does not restrict us to starting at the top or bottom of a set or counting from the left or the right. The starting point could be any object in an array. However, for younger children who are just picking up counting, our example might be a good, easy starting exercise for exploring order irrelevance.

Understanding these two principles also suggests that the child recognizes three key ideas about counting. First, the counting item (e.g., an apple) is an object rather than a number label/tag (an aspect of the abstraction principle—for example, the number word *one* can be tagged to any object, not only to an apple). Second, verbal tags are only temporarily assigned to objects until the end of the counting sequence (i.e., the object counted as *two* when objects are counted from one side of the set could have another number assigned to it if you start counting in another direction). Third, the same cardinal/last number tag results regardless of the order in which objects are counted.

Competency in numbers requires that young children understand and implement all five counting principles. We recommend that children be encouraged to start counting at the number one when they are initially learning to count and until they have demonstrated a sound understanding of at least the first three counting principles. Only after the counting principles are firmly in place for numbers up to 5 and then 10 should children be encouraged to count starting from any other number, such as counting from the number two or counting by twos. Children are capable of starting school with a firm understanding of numbers up to 10 if they learn the counting principles we just discussed (Baroody & Wilkins, 1999; Fuson, 1988).

Gallistel and Gelman (1990) have argued that these counting principles are innate—that children come hardwired for counting. Indeed, there is lots of evidence to support that humans have some innate capacity for numbers (Butterworth, 1999a; 1999b; Dehaene, Molko, Cohen, & Wilson,

||||||| TEXT BOX 3.3.   ORDER IRRELEVANCE

Adult: Let's count the rings from the bottom.

Child: One, two, three, four.

Adult: That's great! Are we going to get the same number if we count from the top? Let's try that.

Child: One, two, three, four!

Adult: Yes, it's the same number. It's four!

2004; Dehaene, Spelke, Stanescu, Pinel, & Tsivkin, 1999). However, more recent evidence suggests that actually *learning* to count numbers requires some additional environmental contributions (Le Corre, Van de Walle, Brannon, & Carey, 2006). This more recent evidence emphasizes the importance of providing meaningful and intentional opportunities to engage with numbers early on in a child's life. This intentional engagement has been shown to be very important for mathematical achievement (Curtis, Okamoto, & Weckbacher, 2009).

The mathematical learning process is slightly different from literacy, which is also thought to have some innate components. Adults do not stop and teach young children about sentence structure, yet children start speaking in complex sentences without actually being taught about verbs, nouns, and so forth. This phenomenon does not appear with numbers. The development of a complex under- standing of numbers does not just happen without some environmental input from adults.

Brain imaging research shows some of the lasting impacts of developing these early counting skills. Researchers looking at the brains of senior high school students have found that the brain regions responsible for basic mathematical concepts, such as counting, are the very same ones responsible for more complex mathematics skills involved in algebra, complex geometry, or complex arithmetic (Matejko, Price, Mazzocco, & Ansari, 2013). Matejko and colleagues found that the regions of the brain responsible for basic mathematics "provide the neuroanatomical scaffold for successful learning of higher-level math skills" (p. 609). In particular, Matejko and colleagues propose that a high level of water diffusion in the white matter of the brain is a good predictor of strong performance on the mathematics subtest of the Preliminary Scholastic Aptitude Test (PSAT), a commonly utilized measure used to predict college achievement. This research provides strong anatomical evidence for the links between early basic number and mathematics knowledge and later achievement.

SYMBOLIC REPRESENTATIONS OF NUMBERS

Between the ages of 2 and 3, young children begin to learn about symbolic representations of numbers, also known as numerals. Drawing from Piaget, Kamii (2000) suggests that symbols usually *look* like what they represent. For example, a picture of an apple represents an apple. However, symbolic representations can also be marks to denote something. For example, a young child may use a circle to represent an apple. In contrast, numerals are symbolic representations of numbers and may represent just about anything. For example, the number symbol "1" could represent someone's age, one apple, one person, and so forth. Young children have to learn not only the number words and what their symbols look like but also their underlying and contextualized meaning of "one-ness" (Moomaw, 2011, p. 25).

Young children learn what the number symbols looks like (e.g., "2") and the names of numbers (e.g., *two*) by seeing numbers and having them named by others (Cross, Woods, & Schweingruber, 2009). Learning the symbolic representations up to the number nine is remarkably easy for young children, although some mix up symbols such as "2" and "5" and "6" and "9" because of their similarities in appearance (Baroody & Wilkins, 1999). Using analogies such as "8 is like a snowman" and routinely identifying numbers in everyday settings help children learn numerals. Most children should be able to identify any of the counting numbers in symbolic form (i.e., "1, 2, 3, 4, 5, 6, 7, 8, 9") by the start of formal schooling. Some children have the manual dexterity to be able to write some of the numbers by the age of 3 but some start as late as age 6, depending on their early childhood environment (Clements & Sarama, 2009, p. 26). Writing numbers is something that children should be encouraged to do, and children may need some direct support in writing their first numbers.

Recognizing the symbolic representation of a number may be independent of understanding the cardinality that number represents or understanding the relationship of a number to the other numbers in the counting sequence. For example, a child may be able to rote or verbally count to two, give you two objects when asked for two (thus having an understanding of cardinal meaning), and respond *two* when asked how many (i.e., cardinal word), but he or she still may not recognize the numerical symbol "2" as the number "*two*." Young children's complete understanding of various representations of numbers across different contexts (e.g., a number used in a cardinality setting and then used in a symbolic setting) happens rapidly as counting develops between ages 2 and 4.

LITTLECOUNTERS

Developed in 2009, the LittleCounters (Kotsopoulos & Lee, 2012) is a community-based workshop consisting of five 45-minute sessions that focuses on introducing adults who either work with or care for children (i.e., early childhood caregivers or educators or grandparents) or have children (i.e., parents) to the importance of early mathematics learning. The five counting principles identified by Gallistel and Gelman (1990) are one of the backbones of our workshops because of their foundational role in mathematics learning. The workshops are interactive and adults can attend them with a child (or children). We model and introduce early mathematical concepts through purposeful play (as discussed in the previous chapter) among parents, caregivers, and early childhood educators and children using toys, games, songs, stories, and poems.

Although young children also participate in the workshops, the main goal of LittleCounters is to show adults how to include mathematical learning in a child's play or daily interactions through the use of songs, games, stories, and movements. The workshops focus on supporting the development of each of the counting principles (i.e., stable order, one-to-one correspondence, order irrelevance, cardinality, and abstraction). Each of the five sessions also focuses on other mathematical concepts such as symbolic representations of numbers, magnitude (more or less), ordinal numbers (first, second, third), ordinality (small to large, left to right), and parity (equal or the same). See Appendix A for a more detailed description of the sessions and for suggested activities that can be used to develop each of the counting principles and these additional concepts.

We stress that LittleCounters is not and should not be thought of as a curriculum for early childhood mathematics. Nor is it meant to be an intense intervention program for the development of counting skills. As we discussed earlier, the developmental continuum between early counting and an understanding of cardinality of larger sets takes approximately a year. As such, it is not possible to trigger such rapid growth of mathematical skills over the course of five sessions.

Instead, LittleCounters is geared toward adults engaging with young children who may not have the background knowledge of counting principles and early mathematical cognition and who might not know easy ways to talk and play with mathematics with their children. This workshop is meant for individuals who 1) have direct contact with and care for young children in either a home, child care, or early learning setting and 2) have limited prior knowledge of early mathematical cognition. This book is an outgrowth of the LittleCounters workshop, and we hope it will support adults by facilitating a deeper understanding of numbers, counting, and early mathematical cognition in relatively easy and accessible ways. Understanding and incorporating these easy and accessible concepts will undoubtedly have a tremendous impact on the mathematical development of young children.

There are several key educational and developmental approaches that we model for the adults in our LittleCounters workshops: 1) using developmentally appropriate countable sets (e.g., with younger kids, using no more than three or four objects); 2) beginning with counting forward before counting backward; 3) using "Name It, Show It (and Say It), Touch It (and Say It), Move It (and Say It), Say It" as a guiding framework for modeling counting with young children; and 4) emphasizing counting everything and anything.

Another main point worth highlighting is that LittleCounters does not advocate direct teaching. Indeed, the very nature of these interactive sessions is in direct contrast with direct teaching. As we explain in Chapter 2, play should belong to the child. Adults are reminded to be conscious of the potential for contaminating play by interfering with the child's own spontaneous play in order to increase mathematical engagement with the child. During the LittleCounters workshops, we do initiate games for the purpose of modeling the concepts. However, we stress the importance of picking up on the spontaneous moments that emerge from play rather than directly influencing play, as we must do during the individual sessions in order to model the ideas for the adults.

The games and activities suggested or modeled during the workshop are meant to provide some "how-to" ideas for adults, as well as to dispel doubt or anxiety adults might have that "teaching" early mathematical concepts such as counting to young children through play and daily interactions is difficult. In fact, the feedback that we have received from all adults who attended our workshops was that introducing mathematical talk and activities during play was much easier than they imagined. Participants in these workshops have also told us that they were provided with useful, research-based information on early mathematical development and practical tips and suggestions to promote early mathematical learning.

With these points in mind, we will now discuss the four key educational and developmental approaches highlighted in our LittleCounters workshop.

Developmentally Appropriate Countable Sets

Research suggests that children begin to understand the cardinal (i.e., quantity) meanings of *one* and *two* by about 24 months of age. This also coincides with knowing the number words (Wynn, 1990). Evidence from our own research shows that children as young as 20 months have an understanding of the number one prior to rote counting aloud (Lee, Kotsopoulos, Tumber, & Makosz, forthcoming).

In the first session of our LittleCounters workshop, we always start by asking adults to take out what they think is a developmentally appropriate number of chain-link counters to prepare for the first play activity. Adults very often overestimate the number of objects their child is able to count. Often, the basis of this overestimation is a false illusion of understanding that stems from a child's ability to either identify symbolic representations of numbers or rote count well into the double digits. As we discussed previously, the developmentally appropriate quantities for counting activities for young children are initially quite small (i.e., fewer than three).

We have often observed parents, caregivers, and early childhood educators trying to count with children with sets of objects that are too large—for example, using a pile of 10 or more objects to count with a 2-year-old child! Using too many objects can distract or overwhelm a young child and should be avoided. Always start with sets of objects that are countable for your child. If you are not sure how high your child can really count, always start with a set of three or even two.

Be sure that your child can count the small set of objects and observe to see if he or she can consistently demonstrate the first three counting principles (one-to-one correspondence, stable order, and cardinality) before you increase the number of objects the child is counting. As a guiding principle, lean toward using the maximum number of objects with which he or she has already demonstrated an understanding of one-to-one correspondence, cardinality, and stable order. Text Box 3.4 lists a simple procedure for checking how much a child understands the counting principles for a given set.

Forward Counting First

Have you ever read a counting book that started from the number 10 and then worked backward? Have you ever sang a song or read a poem that focused on backward number counting? Have you ever engaged in a "countdown" with a child to get him or her ready for a nap, a change in activities, departures, or imaginative play with the launch of aircraft? Many of us use counting backward activities with young children—sometimes even routinely. However, we have to ask ourselves whether or not it makes sense to do so if the child has yet to master counting forward.

There are many songs and storybooks that count backward (e.g., "Five little monkeys jumping on a bed . . . four little monkeys jumping on a bed"), and children have been shown to be able to count backward around the age of 5 (Clements & Sarama, 2009, p. 29). Although counting backward activities are useful and important, we discourage using these activities until your child can easily demonstrate the first three counting principles (one-to-one correspondence, stable order, and cardinality) for sets of objects up to 10.

There has not been any research that we know of that explores whether engaging in counting backward too early on is problematic for early mathematical learning. It may be that it has no direct impact. However, the analogy we often share with the adults in our workshops is that

---

 TEXT BOX 3.4. CHECKING FOR COUNTING

- Take five similar objects that a child can count, such as toy cars, blocks, and figures.
- Ask the child to count the objects and listen for stable order.
- Ask the child to tell you how many objects he or she just counted.
- Ask the child to give you five of the objects.
- Try this again with another set of different objects, perhaps during other play at a later time.
- Did the child do all the tasks again correctly? If so, try the same sequence of activities with a total of 10 objects if the child already has been rote counting to 10 and beyond.

counting backward before mastering forward counting is like learning to drive a car in reverse when you have yet to manage driving forward. In addition, counting backward requires children to understand the ordering and relationship among numbers, such as how four comes before three in backward counting because four is actually one *more* than three. Unless the child has a good understanding of the cardinal meaning of number words and their relationship to numbers, we strongly suggest the child be encouraged to start counting forward first.

Using Fingers and Gestures to Count

Most of us use our hands, including fingers, while we converse with others. Such hand movements are known as gestures. It is common for us to touch, tap, or even point at an object while we talk. Gestures play two essential roles in learning. First, gestures serve to convey one's thoughts that may not be adequately expressed in words (Goldin-Meadow, 2005; Sfard, 2009). Second, gestures serve to enhance joint attention between one or more individuals to direct focus on a particular object (e.g., using fingers during counting), an idea (e.g., pointing at a puzzle piece during puzzle construction), or a concept (e.g., building a structure; Reynolds & Reeve, 2001).

Finger counting is a form of gesturing. Fingers have always played an important role in learning to count and counting. Fingers hold a unique one-to-one relationship to objects being counted— particularly for small sets. Sets of objects up to 10 can be represented using both sets of fingers. Regardless of the age of the individual, finger counting should not be discouraged. In addition to the compelling evidence linking fingers to counting and mathematical learning, fingers (and, for some, even toes) are an everpresent object set that can be used for counting.

Many individuals continue to use finger representations of quantities into adulthood when trying to keep track of counted objects. Adults almost intuitively use fingers and various other gestures (e.g., pointing, tapping) when counting with their young children. Finger counting is a very common gesture that children in all cultures use, and many children use finger counting before even receiving formal instruction in mathematics (Butterworth, 1999a). In some cultures, such as India, finger counting is actually taught to children between the ages of 3 and 7 years old before they enter formal schooling. However, some differences may exist between cultures in the ways some numbers are represented with fingers (Cross et al., 2009, p. 133). For example, there are at least three different ways to represent the number "*three*." (See Figure 3.2.)

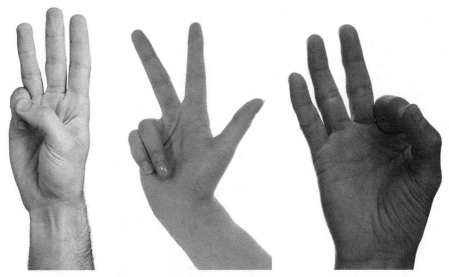

Figure 3.2.   Fingers counting to three.

Finger counting has been shown to be an important and crucial early physical representation of numbers for children (Butterworth, 1999b; 2005). Remarkably, finger gnosis, or the ability to recognize one's own fingers, has been found to be a unique predictor of number system knowledge and calculation skills in first grade students (Penner-Wilger et al., 2007). One study conducted by Fayol, Barrouillet, and Marinthe (1998) found that finger gnosis at age 5 predicts children's mathematical competence 3 years later! Not everyone can recognize his or her own fingers. Testing for finger gnosis can be done using a variety of methods. One method involves hiding a person's hand from view and then lightly touching his or her fingers below the knuckle to see if the person recognizes which finger has been touched (Noël, 2005). Another method involves asking individuals to recognize representations of counting on their own or other people's fingers (Butterworth, 1999a; 1999b).

Likewise, finger *agnosia*, the *inability* to recognize fingers, your own or others, has also been reported as an important predictor of children at risk for mathematical difficulties (Andres, Di Luca, & Pesenti, 2008; Penner-Wilger et al., 2007). There seems to be an important mind–body link among the ability to recognize one's own fingers, represent numbers with fingers, and understand numbers. Thus the use of gestures such as finger counting is crucial in learning early mathematical concepts such as number sense, especially for children 2–6 years old (Gracia-Bafalluy & Noël, 2008; Saxe & Kaplan, 1981).

Some suggest that the finger counting gesture is the link between the preverbal and verbal representational systems of numbers (Andres, Di Luca, & Pesenti, 2008; Fayol & Seron, 2005). That is, the acquisition of numerical concepts, such as the counting principles involving language, is facilitated by the use of fingers. This theory is based on observations of children's spontaneous use of their fingers while counting and empirical studies supporting the relationship between the ability to represent numbers through finger counting and the acquisition of numerical knowledge. For example, it has been observed that children use their fingers in a consistent order—using either the thumb or the little finger as the starting base—during counting. This has led to the conclusion that finger counting gestures help young children to acquire counting principles such as the one-to-one mapping correspondence between the physical objects and the mental representations of numerosity and the stable order (Andres, Di Luca, & Pesenti, 2008).

The close relationship between the use of fingers and numerical knowledge is further supported by neuroscience studies conducted with adults. These studies reveal that gesturing in the form of finger counting and activating numerical representations involve the same brain areas (Andres, Olivier, & Badets, 2008; Andres, Seron, & Olivier, 2007; Pesenti, Thioux, Seron, & De Volder, 2000). This supports the hypothesis put forth by Butterworth (1999a), who suggested that "without the ability to attach number representations to the neural representations of fingers and hands in their normal locations, the numbers themselves will never have a normal representation in the brain" (pp. 249–250).

One of the books we read during our LittleCounters workshops is one of two books that we have written, titled *LittleCounters® at the Market* (Lee & Kotsopoulos, 2012). The second book is called *LittleCounters® around the World Count* (Kotsopoulos & Lee, in press). These counting books have some unique features not commonly found in children's counting books. First, each page has a picture of a hand depicting the finger representation of the number along with the symbolic representation of the number. Second, a nonsymbolic representation of the number in relation to other numbers along a number line is also included. Objects and shapes depicted in the books are mostly familiar to children. This way, the children can relate what they learned about counting with objects from the book to their own environment and context. A sample of the representation of the number one in our first book can be seen in Figure 3.3.

Children have been found to count more accurately when counting is accompanied by gestures such as pointing or touching and either their own or another person's gestures (Alibali & DiRusso, 1999). Graham (1999), in his study of counting accuracy in 2- to 4-year-olds, found that children who were able to demonstrate consistent evidence of the one-to-one principal of counting (i.e., each object counted only once) used gestures to point to objects. In this study, the use of a pointing gesture during counting was also found to be related to counting accuracy. Other studies report that a touching gesture is more effective than pointing during counting (Alibali & DiRusso, 1999; Gelman & Meck, 1983).

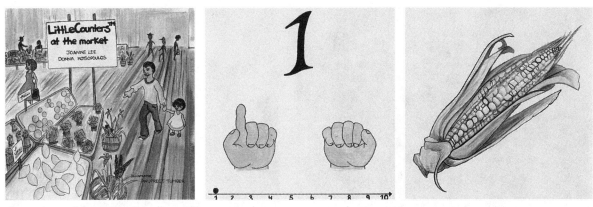

Figure 3.3. *LittleCounters® at the market.*

Our recent research has shown the five most frequent types of gestures produced by parents playing with their toddlers are grouping objects in a set, counting objects while enumerating, tapping/touching, holding up an item, and pointing at an item (Figure 3.4; Lee et al., in press). These gestures happened while the parent–child pairs were engaging in mathematical talk and activities. We also found that toddlers whose parents use more of these five types of gestures produced more of these gestures themselves (see Figure 3.4). Another recent study from our lab revealed that the use of counting object gestures while counting out loud by children between 18 and 41 months old predicted their mathematical competence a year later (Lee, Kotsopoulos, Tumber, & Makosz, forthcoming).

Name It, Show It (and Say It), Touch It (and Say It), Move It (and Say It), Say It

A child may be more able to demonstrate his or her counting principles if the countable objects are organized in a way that lessens the potential of the arrangement to be distracting by, for example, spacing them evenly apart. The appropriate arrangement of counting objects can also reduce the likelihood of repeat or double counting, because most young children do not intuitively know to separate objects to make the objects easier to distinguish (Figure 3.5).

A key strategy that we model and advocate for during counting with young children in our LittleCounters workshop is "Name It, Show It (and Say It), Touch It (and Say It), Move It (and Say It), Say It." Here is how it works: Start with a developmentally appropriate set of objects. Count the objects. Name the number of objects you are about to count (*name it*); show the number with your fingers and count the objects (*show it*); touch or point to the objects as you count them (*touch it and say it*); move the objects as you count them to recreate the set of objects a short distance away (*move it and say it*); say the cardinality (*say it*). See Figure 3.6.

From our observations working with the children and adults in our LittleCounters workshop, children develop the one-to-one counting principle faster and are able to demonstrate this understanding faster when recreating the set a short distance away from the original set. By moving the object over, touching it, and naming it, there is less chance of repeat counting of objects. These steps provide good physical cues for young children to keep track of what objects have been counted and what have not.

This "Name It, Show It (and Say It), Touch It (and Say It), Move It (and Say It), Say It" strategy incorporates the results of a body of research that shows that 1) attaching words to numbers supports building an understanding of the numbers (Huang, Spelke, & Snedeker, 2010), 2) multiple representations of numbers enhances learning (Freeman, Antonucci, & Lewis, 2000; Goldin & Kaput, 1996; Penner-Wilger et al., 2009; Rasmussen & Bisanz, 2005), and 3) gesturing helps facilitate understanding about numbers and counting (Alibali & DiRusso, 1999; Cook & Tanenhaus, 2009; Goldin-Meadow, Cook, & Mitchell, 2009; Graham, 1999; Saxe & Kaplan, 1981).

1. Grouping objects

2. Counting objects while enumerating

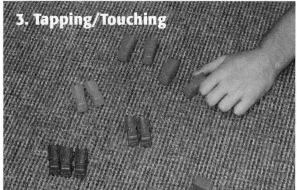

3. Tapping/Touching

5. Pointing

4. Holding up an item

Figure 3.4. Types of gestures.

Harder to count

Easier to count

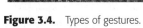

Figure 3.5. Harder and easier to count.

Name it.	Show it (& Say it).	Touch it (& Say it).	Move it(& Say it).	Say it.
"Two."	"One. Two."	"One. Two."	"One. Two."	"Two."

Figure 3.6. Name It, Show It (and Say It), Touch It (and Say It), Move It (and Say It), Say It.

Count Everything and Anything

Everything is countable! The key to purposeful play is that you can take any daily activity or outing and make it playful in ways that enhance and support learning in mathematics, language, or science. With young children, building counting and number talk into everyday activities is much easier than you may think! Things to count could include the following:

· Food items (e.g., apple slices, rice grains, raisins, cereal, sips, snacks, spoonfuls)

· Bubbles, rubber ducks, fish, or scoops of water in the bathtub

· Steps and jumps

· Stairs and flooring tiles

· Body parts, such as hands and feet (especially when getting dressed)

· Toys or even household items, such as plates or sippy cups

· Elements in nature (e.g., puddles, flower petals, squirrels, bunny rabbits)

· Time (e.g., minutes, days)

· Family members and pets

In Text Box 3.5, Danny makes counting a fun part of his father-son outing by catching tadpoles and explaining how they become frogs when they grow older. We can see from their exchange that Harley does not quite have a rational understanding of the number two, because when his dad scoops up some more tadpoles, he again says, "Two tadpoles." This repetitive behavior is not actually counting or recognizing objects as counting. Here, we can see that Harley understands the quantity aspect of objects (that there are more), and as such, he responds with a number. We also know that when the two count the tadpoles, Harley does not exhibit one-to-one correspondence or stable order. That being said, it would be hard to try to count one-to-one with tadpoles swimming in someone's hands! What we are trying to illustrate here is that counting and initiating conversations about counting can happen anywhere, even on a nature trail. Such interactions, whether inside or outside the comfort of home, can lead to some important insights about a child's developmental progression toward counting.

TEXT BOX 3.5.   CATCHING TADPOLES

Danny and his 2-year-old son, Harley, love to visit the Laurel Creek. When the creek is running fairly slowly on a sunny spring day, it is easy to stand at the banks and catch tadpoles. Danny bends down and scoops up some water in his cupped hands. Harley is delighted to see two tadpoles swimming in his dad's hands. He squeals with delight! Danny says, "Two tadpoles! Let's catch some more." He scoops up some more water, and in his palm are several small tadpoles. Harley yells, "Two tadpoles!" Danny says, "It looks like there are more than two tadpoles! Let's try to count them." Harley begins to count, skipping a couple of numbers but getting to six before reaching in to try to scoop some tadpoles from his dad's hands.

We encourage you to make counting part of your child's everyday activities—be it on a nature trail; in corn mazes; or at the beach, golf club, or skating rink. The things that are countable are endless! In Chapter 6, we will discuss in more detail how to include counting, number talk, and mathematics in everyday routines and activities.

CHAPTER SUMMARY

It is not surprising to see that children entering first grade are able to rote count up to double-digit numbers but are unable to show an understanding of one-to-one correspondence (i.e., they count the same objects twice), cardinality, or stable-order principles. Rote counting creates an illusion of competency that can seriously hinder a child's learning potential. This does not have to be the case. Children can, during their first few years of life, engage in play related to counting that increases their mathematical understanding. Parents, caregivers, and early childhood educators can mathematize elements of play and use language purposefully to draw children's attention to counting and numbers in their daily interactions and activities.

Children can understand numbers one and two very early on in life and are capable of counting and understanding numbers up to 10 prior to formal schooling. The "Name It, Show It (and Say It), Touch It (and Say It), Move It (and Say It), Say It" strategy incorporates both language and gestures. This has been shown to be a powerful combination for facilitating the learning of counting and numbers, even for students at the grade-school level.

Unlike reading, numeracy is put aside until children start formal schooling. Studies looking at Asian countries and even North America have shown that children who have exposure to early counting experiences do better in mathematics when they start school (Duncan et al., 2007; Miller, Kelly, & Zhou, 2005). There is also strong evidence that rational counting can influence academic achievement in mathematics from the very start of formal schooling right through to college. Counting can and should be part of a child's everyday experience.

Chapter 4

Let's Talk About Numbers!

If you are a parent of a young child or if you work with young children, take a moment to think about the content of the talks you have with them during your daily interactions. What probably comes to mind when you think about these daily talks is the frequent use of words associated with objects and places (nouns), some action words (verbs), and some descriptive words (adjectives). But how about the use of mathematical words, such as one, two, *and* three *(number words) and* how many, more, *and* fewer *(quantity words)?*

Adults and children talk about all sorts of things. Sometimes the child initiates the discussion, and sometimes it is the parent. Children often come home and have conversations about things they did at school, but they rarely include details about engaging and fun mathematics. Conversations about numbers and mathematics in everyday contexts are not that typical. However, these are precisely the kinds of conversations that have been shown to have a big impact on young children's understanding of mathematics and their achievement once they enter formal schooling (Gunderson & Levine, 2011; Klibanoff, Levine, Huttenlocher, Vasilyeva, & Hedges, 2006). What sorts of conversations can you imagine having with young children based on numbers, counting, and mathematics?

WHAT IS MATHEMATICAL TALK?

In this book and our LittleCounters program, one of our goals is to show adults how to increase mathematically relevant input/talk with young infants, toddlers, and preschoolers during their daily interactions. This is not to be mistaken for advocating formal instruction of mathematical concepts by planning a curriculum or by constant "math talk." Instead, we are encouraging adults, be it parents, grandparents, caregivers, or early childhood educators (ECEs), to make a conscious effort to talk about mathematical concepts, such as quantity or size, just as they would talk about a house, car, or flowers in their daily interactions. Mathematical talk is simply using number or quantity words to talk about everyday things. Text Box 4.1 lists some examples of number words you can incorporate into daily conversations with young children.

A familiar example with breakfast cereal can illustrate our point here. Typically, a parent or caregiver might name or label a cereal such as Cheerios for a child but might not use number words such as "One Cheerio, two Cheerios" when the child is putting the Cheerios into his or her mouth. What we are suggesting here is that we make learning mathematics an engaging activity that is included in our daily lives. This approach encourages children to make guesses, question, and justify their own and others' observations and think about numbers in their environment. This practical way of approaching

---

 TEXT BOX 4.1. EXAMPLES OF MATH WORDS

Counting

- Numbers: one, two, three, four, and so forth
- Ordering: first, second, third, fourth, fifth, sixth, seventh, eighth, ninth, tenth

Comparing and describing

- Bigger than
- Smaller than
- Less than
- Same
- Half
- Some
- More
- Equal
- A lot

---

mathematical learning, as opposed to more detached ways of doing mathematics such as completing a set of worksheets, might prevent some children from gradually learning to avoid things involving mathematics or even developing mathematical anxieties or phobias.

WHAT DO PARENTS TALK ABOUT WITH THEIR YOUNG CHILDREN?

Parents use relatively less mathematical talk with their young children than other types of talk (e.g., talk related to books, use of nouns, object naming). Our research revealed that English-speaking parents used less than 5% mathematical words in 30-minute play sessions with their children at home (Lee, Kotsopoulos, & Tumber, 2010; Lee, Kotsopoulos, & Tumber, forthcoming). Moreover, parents engage in more naming of objects than actions with their toddlers during their play sessions—in other words, they use more object names (nouns) than action words (verbs; Lavin, Hall, & Waxman, 2006; Tardif, Shatz, & Naigles, 1997).

A possible reason for the infrequent mathematical talk observed at home or even in child care centers is that parents, caregivers, and ECEs in North America tend to place more emphasis on literacy skills than on numeracy skills (Tudge & Doucet, 2004). Many adults view mathematics as an academic subject that should be left to the teachers once children start formal schooling. We also need to bear in mind that many of us are not comfortable with mathematics. This is evidenced by the Adult Literacy and Life Skills Survey in 2005, which indicated that 50% of Canadian adults ages 16 to 65 lacked the minimum mathematical literacy skills necessary to cope with the everyday demands of an advanced society (Statistics Canada, 2005). In order to equip our younger generation with basic and even advanced mathematical skills, we advocate a new way of thinking about mathematics.

Several studies over the last few years have explored the implications of exposing young children to number talk. Given that the environment is the number one contributor to a child's development, this recent interest in number talk is an important shift in thinking about ways to support young children in their development and readiness for schooling. One recent study by researchers Elizabeth Gunderson and Susan Levin (2011) looked closely at the types of number talk parents engage in with their young children at home and the implications of this number talk for young children's understanding of cardinality (the total number of a set of objects counted). Families in this study were visited in their homes once every 4 months and had children between the ages of 14 and 30 months. During these visits, routine interactions were recorded and later analyzed for the parents' use of number talk. For example, the researchers counted the number words a parent used when picking up his or her child: "One, two, three, up!" Another example could be if, when reading, a parent used language to denote quantity, such as "We never really get through one whole story." In this case, the word "whole" would have been considered number talk used by the parents (p. 1025). At the conclusion of the study, children were tested on a cardinality task that asked them to identify pictures of quantities of up to six objects. Gunderson and Levin's findings show that the more number talk used by parents, particularly when counting or labeling sets of objects that were present and visible in the home environment, the better the children's later cardinal-number knowledge. In addition, parents' use of number talk that was slightly beyond what might be developmentally appropriate (e.g., quantities of 7 to 10 objects) encouraged a greater knowledge of cardinal numbers in their children—more so than those that used smaller set sizes more routinely.

Gunderson and Levin's (2011) findings support the idea of a zone of proximal development, which we discussed in Chapter 2, and the practice of thinking intentionally about where the child might go next in terms of his or her learning progression. Using number talk that includes some talk just beyond the child's current developmental range can be seen as an implementation of the development-enhancing feature we discussed in Chapter 2 to help the child move along in his or her own zone of proximal development.

Likewise, a study of preschoolers in a child care setting by Klibanoff and colleagues (2006) found a strong positive relationship between the amount of mathematical input from preschool teachers and the growth of children's mathematical knowledge during the year. These researchers showed that the more mathematical talk the teachers used, the more mathematical knowledge the children acquired. The evidence from both the home and the early child care and learning centers points to the fact that talking about numbers, mathematical concepts, and counting all enhance young children's mathematical development.

What matters in your home or the early child care center you are affiliated with? Is there evidence of numbers and mathematical thinking proudly displayed and available as conversation starters? Are parents and caregivers aware of the fact that mathematics learning is happening and can even advance further in the home? Frances' efforts in her center are not common, as illustrated in Text Box 4.2. Evidence of literacy and art in the hallways and classrooms of early learning centers is quite common. However, although most ECEs, caregivers, and parents think mathematics is important, they do not fully understand its role in early childhood development (Sarama & Clements, 2009).

 TEXT BOX 4.2.   SHOW ME THE NUMBERS

Frances supervises a regional early child care center. She has been encouraging a focus on both literacy and numeracy at her center. When you arrive at the center, you immediately see a large number mural in the hallway. Next to each doorway in the school, there are "math walls," and in every classroom, there are "math word walls" where new mathematical terms that are being learned are posted. Twice a week, the center has "gallery walks," where children walk with their class through the halls and admire one another's work in literacy and numeracy. The gallery walks allow the children to see each other's work and notice how their friends are thinking. The gallery walks also give each early childhood educator (ECE) the opportunity to see what others are doing in their classes. Many of the educators often express surprise at the amount of mathematics happening even in the toddler classroom!

The implications of the existing research on early childhood numeracy and its impacts on future learning and understanding of mathematics are clear. Children who are exposed to mathematical talk in early childhood have been shown to do better in various areas of mathematics, such as counting, basic arithmetic, and spatial reasoning (Ferrara, Hirsh-Pasek, Newcombe, Golinkoff, & Lam, 2011; Gunderson & Levine, 2011; Klibanoff et al., 2006; Pruden, Levine, & Huttenlocher, 2011).

Though this chapter is focused on number talk, spatial talk is also important in early mathematics development. The use of spatial language by parents has also been studied in the homes of young children (and in a lab setting too), and the results are similar to those just reported for number talk. In particular, parents who use more spatial language have children who also use more spatial language (Cannon, Levine, & Huttenlocher, 2007; Ferrara et al., 2011; Pruden et al., 2011). More important, these children perform better on spatial reasoning tasks compared with children whose parents did not use spatial language frequently (Cannon et al., 2007; Pruden et al., 2011). Spatial language during puzzle play, for example, was found to be important for developing young children's use of spatial language and spatial reasoning (Cannon et al., 2007). An example of spatial language can be seen in Text Box 4.3.

The kind of language (see roman text) that James uses in Text Box 4.3 is an example of the spatial language that we are discussing and is easy enough for most adults to incorporate with some purposeful effort. Engaging young children between 3 and 6 years old in activities related to numeracy and geometry during play or daily interactions is highly recommended by the National Research Council Committee on Early Childhood Mathematics (National Research Council, 2005).

TALKING AND LEARNING ABOUT NUMBERS

Numbers and relationships between numbers can be found everywhere and in our everyday interactions. Daily tasks, such as knowing how many guests are coming for dinner in order to set the table or deciding which of two plates has more cookies, require a good understanding of one-to-one correspondence and quantity comparison (e.g., more or less). Such daily encounters with mathematics in one's environment present interesting and practical teachable moments.

This informal mathematical knowledge is what Ginsberg (2010) calls "everyday math knowledge," which serves as a foundation for learning formal mathematical knowledge when children start formal schooling. For example, studies have shown that the informal learning of number

 TEXT BOX 4.3.   HELP WITH THE PUZZLE!

James and his 3½-year-old daughter, Mary, are working on a puzzle together. It is the first jigsaw puzzle of this complexity that Mary has done. She loves puzzles, and James thought she was ready and that this would be a fun, quiet activity for them to do together after dinner every day. Although Mary is thrilled when she finds a piece and gets it to fit on her own, often James will find a piece and pass it to Mary for her to place into the puzzle. James looks quickly for the four corners and finds them first. He says to Mary, "This puzzle is rectangular—like the box it came in. We should find the four corners first so that we can use them to help build the shape of the puzzle." *Quickly, the two of them sort through the pieces and find the four corners. He reminds Mary that they are looking for four pieces that have two straight edges each. He finds one and shows it to her to serve as a reminder of what to look for. The next piece James finds fits into one of the corners. He passes it to Mary and says, "It might fit in the* top, left corner piece." *Mary tries to put it in, and James, who is attentive to her actions, says, "You might have to* turn or rotate it *to the other end to get it to fit, Mary." Mary turns the piece in her hands and tries lining it up again with the corner piece.*

concepts before children enter kindergarten is strongly related to number knowledge development, which in turn is a strong predictor of arithmetic achievement in first grade (e.g., Baker et al., 2002).

There are research findings that strongly support the belief that mathematical talk facilitates the learning of mathematical concepts, as evidenced in some of the studies we have already described. First, early mathematical representations such as numerosity (1 unit or 2 units of something) are linked to mathematics language, the knowledge of counting words such as *one* and *two* (e.g., Huttenlocher, Jordan, & Levine, 1994; Jeong & Levine, 2005). Furthermore, many studies in language acquisition have shown that children's general vocabulary growth is related to the amount of language input they receive (e.g., Hart & Risley, 1992; Naigles & Hoff-Ginsberg, 1995).

It has been found that the size of toddlers' vocabularies at age 2 predicts their subsequent literacy achievement up to age 11 (Lee, 2011). In other words, toddlers with a larger vocabulary consistently outperform their peers who have smaller vocabularies in literacy tasks such as passage comprehension (i.e., the ability to understand the meaning and ideas in a passage of text). These findings point to the fact that the foundation for children's literacy development has to be laid early on—even at 2 years old. The studies highlight the importance of the amount of mathematical talk children receive in their daily lives during the early years of life and the impact of early mathematical talk on children's acquisition of mathematical language and concepts. Mathematical talk lays the groundwork for numeracy development by facilitating both children's understanding of mathematical concepts and the mapping of mathematical language onto such concepts—that is, developing both mathematical skills and the language to express them.

Research in neuroscience has also suggested that the first years of life lay the foundation for a person's later capacity for lifelong learning (Greenough, 1997; Shonkoff, 2009). Would you believe that 700 brain cell connections (also known as synapses) are formed every second during the first few years of our lives (Bourgeois, 1997; Huttenlocher, 1984)? Yes, it is true, but this astonishing rate of new cell connections does not continue forever. Instead, the "use it or lose it" principle applies here—that is, those neural connections that are not used in these early years will be pruned off so that our brains can stay efficient. Consequently, it becomes increasingly more difficult (but not impossible) for us to pick up new skills as we get older.

Because early neural development has been found to be so important for later learning, many scientists have highlighted the importance of providing enriched and safe environments for children during their first few years of life, thus laying a solid foundation for healthy development (cognitive, emotional, physical, and social) over a lifetime (e.g., Heckman, 2004; Shonkoff, 2009). We see the rapid rates at which new connections form in the brains of little ones as another reason we should not confine our talk with young children to simple nouns, verbs, and adjectives. Instead, we should try to enrich our daily interactions with our young children by using more mathematical language, such as number words, quantity words, spatial words, and words describing size or magnitude. Of course, some parents, caregivers, or ECEs might be hesitant to do so, as they may doubt that young children are ready to be introduced to these foundational mathematical concepts.

To dispel this doubt, let us go back to the findings we discussed in Chapter 1 regarding the early understanding of numerosity by 6-month-old infants. Given infants' early sensitivity to numbers, some researchers have proposed that we are born with innate abilities to learn mathematical concepts (Butterworth, 2005; Ginsburg, Cannon, Eisenband, & Pappas, 2006). This proposal is similar to the idea that children are born with an innate ability to learn language without much formal instruction. This brings us to yet another reason we believe that mathematical talk facilitates the learning of mathematical concepts. Just as in language development, mathematical development and learning cannot take place effectively without adult input and support (see Text Box 4.4). Thinking that mathematical learning can wait until formal schooling or that it will happen serendipitously prior to formal schooling is not advisable, because it puts children at a disadvantage for later mathematical learning.

Parents, caregivers, and ECEs need to help little ones make the leap from the preverbal or nonsymbolic representations of mathematical concepts such as numerosity to the verbal and symbolic representations for these concepts (see Figure 4.1). This transition is best done by moving from the

| | | | | | | **TEXT BOX 4.4.   HEY, WHERE DID YOU LEARN THAT?**

Kiere picked up his 2-year-old daughter, Fanoula, from the child care center a little late today. Instead of 5 p.m., he arrived closer to 6 p.m., having told the center he would be a little late. After packing up, they depart for home. When they arrive home, Kiere engages in a conversation with Fanoula as they head into the house: "Daddy was a little late today. I didn't come at the same time." Fanoula holds up her right hand and says, "Daddy come five!" Then she holds up her left hand and says, "Five! Five! Five!" Clapping both hands together, Kiere is delighted! He says, "That's right. Daddy comes at 5 p.m. every day. Five! One, two, three, four, five." Kiere raises his hand to show five fingers too! Amazed that his little girl knows about the number five and her five fingers, Kiere enthusiastically tells Fanoula's mom about Fanoula counting to five. After Fanoula shows her mother her five fingers, Kiere comments, "Where and when did she learn that?"

concrete to the more abstract representations of numbers through language. This is why mathematical talk during play and activity time and daily interactions is crucial.

Providing linguistic labels for mathematical concepts helps young children understand these concepts by requiring them to know the meaning of the mathematical words they hear. For example, children learn the *cardinal* word principle (i.e., the last number in the counting sequence representing the total number of items in the set) and the meanings of all the number words within their counting range *after* acquiring the meanings of the individual number words (Wynn, 1990; 1992a; 1992b). In other words, in learning to count five objects, they first learn the meanings of the number words *one* through *five* and then learn that the word *five* represents the total of their count.

It is not that difficult to provide mathematical-relevant input to young children in our daily interactions. Perhaps we could start by making it a habit to use numbers and mathematical words in sentences such as "You need *two* more puzzle pieces"; "Look, there are *three* balls in this box!"; "How *many* Cheerios do you have in your hand?"; "Which plate has *more*?"; or "Which square is *bigger*?" with little ones during their play activities or even everyday activities such as mealtimes. A sample dialogue incorporating mathematical talk can be seen in Text Box 4.5.

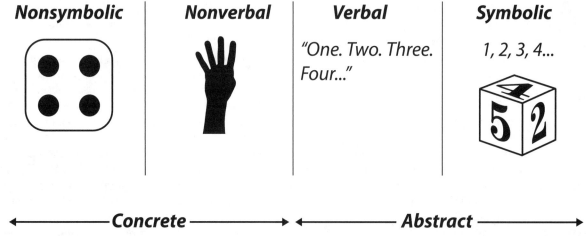

Figure 4.1.   Different representations of numbers.

| | | | | | | **TEXT BOX 4.5.   ONE MORE TOAST, PLEASE**

Addison is 13 months old. She already understands some spoken words, and her mother has also been teaching her sign language. Addison knows how to sign for "more" when she wants more. It is almost lunchtime, and Addison's mom has made her favorite, cheese toast sticks. Addison is playing in her highchair with some toy cubes on her tray. Realizing that lunch is coming by watching her mom getting lunch ready, she tosses one toy cube onto the floor and then another. Seeing this, her mother says, "Addison, did you toss two *blocks onto the floor? Let's see, one, two. Yes, two* blocks on the floor! These go here while you have lunch." She picks up the cubes and puts them on the kitchen table.*

Mom then puts three pieces of cheese toast on Addison's high chair tray and starts to count: "There is one piece of cheese toast. Two pieces of cheese toast. Three pieces of cheese toast. One, two, three! Three pieces of cheese toast for Addison!" She also shows three fingers with her hand. Addison happily starts to eat. She finishes all three pieces and gestures to her mother for more. Addison's mother says, "More?" and gestures back to her. Addison nods excitedly. Addison's mom says, "One more?" and raises one finger on her left hand. Addison looks at her hands and attempts to raise one finger back. Her mom reinforces her efforts by saying "Great job, Addison. That's one!" She then gives Addison another piece of cheese toast.

Another way to add mathematical talk, which is not limited to numbers, to conversations with children is through open-ended questioning. Cross, Woods, and Schweingruber (2009) suggest the following conversation starters (p. 246):

- Where do you see this (mathematical idea) in our classroom?

- Tell me how you figured out (this mathematical idea).

- What is (insert mathematical idea, such as adding or subtracting)?

- What happens if I break this apart/put these together?

- How does this compare with something else? (Which one is smaller/larger? Longer/shorter?)

- Where are the units? What are the units (that children are familiar with)?

- Do you see a pattern? What is the pattern?

In Chapter 6, we talk about including numbers and mathematics in daily routines. Most of us do not think about intentionally counting with young children during activities such as eating, building, or playing with toys. Yet everyday counting seems to have some important implications for children's learning and mathematical development in particular. Focusing on mathematical talk is relatively easy and can bring potentially important learning outcomes for the child.

CHAPTER SUMMARY

This chapter highlights the importance of viewing mathematics as an inclusive part of our environment. Mathematics is not a difficult monster of a subject for young children to learn and is definitely not something that should be left to schoolteachers. Math is everywhere and can be made a part of our daily interactions. By adding mathematically relevant talk with young children into our daily interactions, we are helping them become aware of and understand simple but foundational mathematical concepts. How? This can be done by providing them with a means of representing and mapping mathematical concepts with their language labels via mathematical language. Mathematical language has been shown to be particularly important in the years before formal schooling, and early mathematical language prepares children for later academics (Cross, Woods, & Schweingruber, 2009, pp. 245–246).

5

Other Mathematical Thinking

Is it mathematical? If you are wondering if something a child is doing is mathematical or not, the likely answer is that it is! Have you seen your child build, sort, compare, or guess? These things are all mathematical. Take for example the age-old game of Hide and Seek. A child has to find his or her peer in a space that may or may not be enclosed. He or she must use visual cues, approximations of distance, and a general understanding of area and volume to know, for example, that his or her peer cannot be possibly hiding under a rock. Hide and Seek is fundamentally a game of visual and spatial reasoning and thus mathematical by nature, as are many other games young children play. What other things that you do are mathematical?

The main focus of this book so far has been numbers and fairly simple concepts of numbers and counting. Our focus on this important topic has been motivated by three main points: the ease of incorporating mathematics into everyday activities, the advantages of early mathematical education, and the importance of a solid foundation in basic mathematics for future learning.

Many studies point to the academic advantage children have if they come to school knowing some pretty basic concepts about numbers and counting (Blevins-Knabe & Musun-Miller, 1996; Burchinal et al., 2008; Duncan et al., 2007; Geary, Hoard, Nugent, & Bailey, 2013; La Paro & Pianta, 2000; LeFevre et al., 2009; Romano, Babchishin, Pagani, & Kohen, 2010). These number concepts related to counting are primarily outlined in Chapter 3. These counting concepts are also foundational to many of the other types of mathematical thinking and number sense we will discuss in this chapter (Matejko, Price, Mazzocco, & Ansari, 2013).

Helping children develop a sound understanding of counting and numbers is actually pretty easy if the adult who cares for them understands the counting principles. Most children already have some exposure to counting but perhaps not enough experience with the type of counting that we focus on in this book. Small changes in the way in which adults count with children can have a substantial impact on future academic outcomes.

An understanding of counting and numbers is the cornerstone of all other mathematical knowledge. It lays a foundation to help a child move along a productive trajectory of mathematics learning. In this chapter, we explore a broader view of *number sense*, which is defined as the "interconnected knowledge of numbers and operations" (Cross, Woods, & Schweingruber, 2009, p. 95). Counting and numbers are the groundwork of other types of mathematics (e.g., geometry) and thus our definition of number sense is extended to reflect this perspective: Number sense is the understanding of the relations between number knowledge and numerical operations such as addition or subtraction in a variety of mathematical contexts. If a child does not have a good understanding of counting and numbers, he or she can potentially miss important learning opportunities in numeracy during the first few years of schooling (Byrnes

& Wasik, 2009) but also across most, if not all, mathematics such as measurement, geometry, and so forth.

Counting and numbers are not the only exposure children ought to have to mathematics before starting school. Children engage in all sorts of mathematical tasks in their everyday lives. Sometimes these tasks are recognized as mathematical and other times they are not. In Chapter 2, we described how many of the kinds of play that children engage in spontaneously have mathematical aspects. In our research looking at naturally occurring mathematical language use in families, about 70% of mathematical language was related to counting and number words, and additive/subtractive reasoning and the other 30% was related to shapes (Lee, Kotsopoulos, & Tumber, 2010). Families who participate in LittleCounters have similar proportions of these types of talk but higher numbers of counting and number words overall (Lee et al., 2010).

In this chapter, we discuss other kinds of mathematical thinking that maybe introduced to children before they start school. Each section follows the same format. First, we introduce an explanation of the type of mathematics to be discussed. This is an important first step because it illustrates the simplicity of most of the mathematics we are discussing and how they are appropriate for young children. Even the most reluctant adults know and understand this level of mathematics!

Next, we look at what the research says about what children ought to be able to do prior to formal schooling in terms of each type of mathematics. Parents, caregivers, and early childhood educators want evidence to show that what they are doing can make a difference. Therefore in each section we also report any evidence that suggests there are lasting impacts on children in terms of academic achievement related to that particular type of mathematics.

Finally, for each type of mathematics, we provide some examples of how to introduce the mathematical concept to your child, primarily through the techniques of making mathematics playful, mathematizing play, or telling stories. In some cases, we also draw on everyday routines and activities. Some of the examples we provide in these sections come from activities we engage in during LittleCounters. There are, however, unlimited possibilities for activities to introduce these types of mathematics. When introducing any of these types of mathematics, make an effort to model the numbers, where possible, with your finger representations, and also be sure to use the strategy of "Name It, Show It (and Say It), Touch It (and Say It), Move It (and Say It), Say It."

This chapter is not meant to give you an exhaustive overview of all the mathematical ideas that are appropriate for children under 5 but is rather a sampling of the basic mathematical concepts that can easily be incorporated into a child's early life, with important future implications.

VISUAL SPATIAL REASONING

Visual spatial reasoning is also known to most people as "geometry." It involves manipulating and understanding both 2D (e.g., puzzles) and 3D objects (e.g., blocks), engaging in dynamic geometry (e.g., transformations and rotations of objects in 2D and 3D), and navigating in space through imagined (e.g., via maps) and real whole-body actions (e.g., finding hidden objects in a building). Visual spatial reasoning is not just about shapes! It involves thinking visually, mentally, and even physically about ourselves and objects in our surroundings.

All humans are born into space. We are, by nature, visually and spatially orientated from the beginning of life. This is evident in the results of numerous studies that examined if children can understand visual spatial events prior to having language capabilities. For example, infants as young as 4 months old have been shown to be sensitive to changes in the rotation of objects (Hespos & Rochat, 1997; Rochat & Hespos, 1996).

Some suggest that numbers and visual spatial reasoning should be the central focus of all early childhood mathematics because of their known contributions to future academic success (Newcombe & Frick, 2010). Numeracy and visual spatial reasoning also have fundamental relations to other mathematical concepts and processes that we will discuss in this chapter. Unlike some of the other areas of mathematics, strong evidence already exists on the implications of visual spatial reasoning for increased academic success.

Evidence of links between visual spatial reasoning and mathematics achievement on standardized tests of mathematical ability can be seen by about 3 years of age (Barnes et al., 2011). For example, block play that involves the building of complex structures coupled *with* adult interaction has been shown to predict a child's scores on standardized mathematics testing 1 year later (Lee, Kotsopoulos, & Zambrzycka, 2012). Adults who report engaging in visual spatial activities as a child score higher on visual spatial tasks compared with those who report limited visual spatial activities (Doyle, Voyer, & Cherney, 2012). Furthermore, these adults have better mathematics grades in their 1st year of college.

An important aspect of visual spatial reasoning is that it is highly malleable—individuals can get better at it with education, training, practice, and play (Newcombe & Frick, 2010; Uttal et al., 2013). Puzzles (Levine, Ratliff, Huttenlocher, & Cannon, 2011), storytelling (Casey, Erkut, Ceder, & Young, 2008), spatial language use (Ferrara, Hirsh-Pasek, Newcombe, Golinkoff, & Lam, 2011), and block play (Casey et al., 2008) have all been shown to improve visual spatial reasoning in young children. Storytelling has also been shown to be useful in facilitating visual spatial learning among at-risk populations (Casey et al., 2008).

VISUAL SPATIAL DEVELOPMENT

You may notice that, as your infant grows older, he or she is better at games that involve hidden objects. Although humans are born with the ability to learn how to navigate space, interactions with their local environment and even the start of moving independently contribute to an increased ability to make sense of their physical space.

Navigating Space

How do young children navigate space? By about 6 months of age, young children can remember the movement of an object in relation to them (Acredolo, Adams, & Goodwyn, 1984), and soon after, they can remember routes and paths they have taken in their immediate and familiar environments (Acredolo, 1990). By about 8 months of age, young children demonstrate the ability to take different perspectives and are able to find a hidden object after they have been moved to an alternative location in relation to the object (Bai & Bertenthal, 1992). This ability, also known as *perspective taking,* improves greatly when the child begins to crawl and have independent mobility (Acredolo, 1990; Clearfield, 2004).

Children typically develop the ability to use landmarks and left-right indicators relative to themselves (objects positioned on their left or right side) by about age 2 (Acredolo, 1990; Acredolo & Evans, 1980), although a full understanding of left-right coordinates (e.g., the ability to locate or describe something as located to the left or right) usually develops after age 4 (Cross et al., 2009, p. 187). A good understanding of angles comes later (after age 5; Clements & Sarama, 2009, p. 186).

Giving children instructions for navigating a space, say to find a toy or another object, helps them become more proficient in spatial orientation. Caregivers' use of the "language of space" helps advance children's visual spatial reasoning and spatial language vocabulary (Ferrara et al., 2011; Gunderson & Levine, 2011; Pruden, Levine, & Huttenlocher, 2011). For example, saying "your cup is 'on' the table" or "your bear is 'under' the chair" are ways of introducing different kinds of spatial language that can be useful. These sorts of navigation tasks can also be useful in helping a child develop a spatial or geometric sense of area. Playing with blocks, puzzles, and shape sorters is also very useful and can develop spatial orientation ability, too.

Shapes

Shapes are highly tactile objects and should be in the hands of young children so that they can easily become familiar with them. Starting at about 2 years of age, children can engage in tasks that involve identifying 2D and 3D shapes both generally (e.g., "that's a triangle" and "that's a cube") and also by the properties of the shape (e.g., number of sides, angles; Cross et al., 2009, p. 186; Gershkoff-Stowe & Smith, 2004; Smith, 2009). By about 18–24 months of age, young children are able to identify everyday objects using 3D geometric models that closely resemble the object (Smith, 2009). For example, a toddler can easily recognize and identify a pizza represented by a circle with triangles. At about 22 months of age, toddlers become proficient at shape-sorting games for which objects have to be inserted into holes of matching shapes (Örnkloo & von Hofsten, 2007).

At about the same age, young children can engage in spatial tasks that involve putting shapes together to form other shapes (i.e., composition) or creating other shapes by taking away shapes (i.e., decomposition; Clements, 2004, p. 290; Cross et al., 2009, p. 189). Composition and decomposition with geometric shapes are early forms of proportional reasoning (i.e., fractions, parts of a whole).

Sorting games such as using shape sorters (see Figure 5.1) can be very useful for developing these early competencies in shape recognition. Linking actual objects to shapes is also useful (e.g., a ball is a sphere). When children are encouraged to attend to likenesses or commonalities between the representations of shapes, they become attuned to noticing features that may not be immediately apparent to them: "That's like a triangle but a little different. What's different about it?" (Aslan & Arnas, 2007; Clements, Swaminathan, Hannibal, & Sarama, 1999; Figure 5.2).

In terms of 2D shapes, Clements and colleagues (1999) found that circles were the easiest shapes for preschoolers to identify. These authors propose that young children rely first on the visual matching of features (e.g., "That looks like the square I just had in my hand"), and then, as they grow older, they learn to rely more on the properties of shapes (e.g., four sides, three corners). Shape recognition studies of preschool children at age 3 suggest they cannot yet recognize atypical representations of a shape (e.g., a triangle-like shape with curved sides). Triangles are particularly challenging for preschoolers (Aslan & Arnas, 2007; Clements et al., 1999).

According to Clements (2004, p. 289), by age 4, children can engage in strategies for identifying congruencies (sameness) and symmetries (sameness in parts) in shapes (Figure 5.3).

At about 3½–5 years of age, children can build models that include layouts of rooms or plans of a play area or block construction (Clements & Sarama, 2009, p. 118; Cross et al., 2009, pp. 181–182). Text Box 5.1 illustrates an example of a room layout task.

Figure 5.1. Using "Name It, Show It (and Say It), Touch It (and Say It), Move It (and Say It), Say It" with a shape sorter.

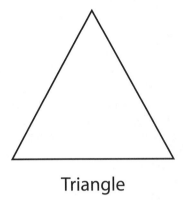

Triangle

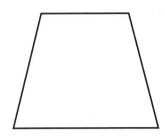

Triangle-like

Figure 5.2. *"That's like a triangle."*

The vignette illustrates the point that although the task itself was about using geometric shapes as representations of real-world objects, children nevertheless may interpret such tasks differently. Moreover, using geometric shapes, such as in the vignette, does not imply an understanding of the shapes. Adults must still engage in purposeful interactions, such as asking questions, to determine what a child knows and is thinking.

Children can also engage in imaginative play related to objects, rotation of objects, or even their perspective in a place. Take, for example, this conversation between an adult and a child:

Adult: Let's play "Guess Where I Am." Close your eyes! I am at a place outside and not too far away from home.

Child: The backyard?

Adult: There is grass under my feet and there is a very tall slide and a very short slide.

Child: The park!

During our LittleCounters workshops, we have adults and children play with a number puzzle to build their spatial abilities. This is a purposeful opportunity to engage in puzzle play, with counting and number symbol recognition. Young children (approximately 2 years old) often need help putting in the puzzle pieces at first but quickly take over from the adult.

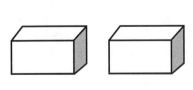

Congruent rectangular prisms

Symmetry: This half of the face is the same as the other half

Figure 5.3. Congruency and symmetry.

| | | | | | | **TEXT BOX 5.1.   PLAN A PLAYGROUND**

As part of a geometry lesson, Ms. Chaktsiris sets up a "plan our playground" in her preschool class. The task involves using various sizes of precut shapes, such as triangles, squares, and rectangles, to create a 2D plan of the playground on a piece of green paper. The children are asked to include in their plans a sandbox (brown rectangles), a splash pad (blue circles), a picnic table (red squares), a climbing area (purple triangle), and trees (green circles). Children are instructed that they can even combine shapes to make, for example, a really big splash pad or sandbox. Orley takes a seat at the table and proceeds to fill the piece of paper with blue circles. Ms. Chaktsiris, noticing that Orley is just using one shape, wanders over and asks about Orley's park plan. Orley responds, "It's not a park. It's water."

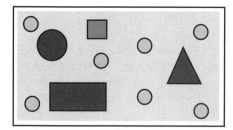 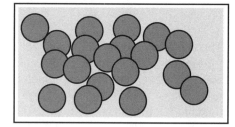

Block Play

Block play is one of the most beneficial forms of visual spatial learning for a young child. Blocks are available in various forms, sizes, and materials. From very early on, when infants start grasping, blocks can and should be introduced—even though they may not be initially used for construction. Infants develop important motor skills by transferring blocks from one hand to another, grasping the blocks, and even passing the blocks to an adult. Blocks also provide opportunities for infants to learn about things in space.

As children begin to develop structures using blocks, adult interaction, the complexity of the structures, and the use of spatial language are particularly important for maximizing the potential benefits of block play. Parents, caregivers, and early childhood educators are encouraged to go beyond simply building a horizontal or vertical stack of blocks (Lee, Kotsopoulos, & Zambrzycka, 2012). Instead, they can engage 1) in connecting two blocks with a third block to form a roof/ bridge over the space between them; 2) in making decorative patterns that follow an AB (e.g., a rectangular block, a cylindrical block), ABA (e.g., a rectangular block, a cylindrical block, a rectangular block), or AABB (e.g., two rectangular blocks followed by two cylindrical blocks) pattern with the shape or color of the blocks; and 3) in representational play, using the block constructions to represent things such as castles or barns. One of our recent studies further reveals that the level of complexity of block play engaged by parents is a good predictor of children's numeracy competence (Lee, Zambrzycka, & Kotsopoulos, forthcoming). Dietze and Kashin (2012) offer some useful ways to start conversations with verbal young children about block play. For instance, you can ask children about the following (p. 197):

- The shape of the blocks you are using

- The blocks on top of, beside …

·   How you got the blocks underneath the …

·   How you made the space for the trucks to go under the bridge …

·   How you can use a plank to connect …

·   How many steps the prince needs to climb to get into the building

·   Why you used squares and triangles in this part of your construction

MEASUREMENT

Measurement connects counting, numbers, and geometry. It is one of the mathematical concepts that we learn as children and continue to use throughout our lives. Children's early exposure to measurement typically involves the use of nonstandard units such as their feet or hands to measure or words such as *more* or *bigger* and then moves to standard units of measurement such as centimeters and inches by about age 4 or 5 (Hiebert, 1981). Some suggest that young children are able to use rulers with some accuracy and may even prefer to use rulers prior to age 5 (Boulton-Lewis, Wilss, & Mutch, 1996). However, even at age 5, children still have trouble identifying the appropriate standard unit of measurement when using a ruler and instead may use visual perception (e.g., "down to there") instead of the units (Boulton-Lewis et al., 1996). Estimation involves approximate values or measures, whereas measurement tends to require more precise methods and values. Much of the research related to measurement can be attributed to the work of Piaget, Inhelder, and Szeminska (1960).

Young children routinely engage in measurement tasks. Probably the most common task that children engage in is measuring their height, which happens for many young children at the doctor's office or in their home and is usually recorded on a chart or even a door frame. When children are asked about their height, it is not uncommon for them to reply "this tall" and point to their head— indicating some sense of where the boundaries of height are within their own physical being. What other sorts of things do young children measure? The list is endless: their height, weight, area, volume, shoe size, time, the height or width of plants, and so forth. Almost anything countable can be measured, including any geometric shape.

Two main challenges young children face with measurement are the concepts of discrete and continuous quantities. For example, given two sets of items of equal length, one having six in the set and the other four units, preschool children will pick the set with six as "longer" despite visual evidence to the contrary (Inhelder, Sinclair, & Bovet, 1974). The discrete number of six is dominant, even with the visual evidence that both lengths are equal. They may also think the length of an object changes if the orientation changes. For example, the same rectangle at 90 degrees may be seen as shorter when it is tilted rectangle at 45 degrees.

Another challenge for young children is the concept of conservation of measurement. Children younger than age 4 will perceive a shift in the volume of a liquid if poured from a smaller to a larger container and will often suggest that there is less liquid once it has been moved to the larger container (Piaget & Inhelder, 1969). Children start to overcome such challenges with conservation of measurement at about the start of formal schooling at age 6 (Vine, 1985). At the start of elementary school, children use fairly rudimentary types of methods to measure length, area, and perimeter and then learn progressively to use more complex methods as they get older (Barrett, Clements, Klanderman, Pennisi, & Polaki, 2006; Outhred & Mitchelmore, 2000; Szilágyi, Clements, & Sarama, 2013). However, other research has reported that children still do not have a sound understanding of measurement even in Grades 3 and above (Kamii, 1997). As Kamii (1997) has shown, even knowing how to align a ruler properly to measure a straight line can be a problem for some elementary school–age children.

During LittleCounters, we engage in a variety of measurement games using nonstandard units of measurement combined with our counting principles. Here are a few things we do:

- We use a poem about a bean sprout that grows and grows "this tall" and then goes pop (see Appendix A for other examples).

- We compare the sizes of our hands by pressing our hands up against those of the children while counting the fingers—"Look I have five fingers and you have five fingers, one, two, three, four, five! We each have five but my hand is bigger!"

- We also do motions to a song about vegetables and fruit on a track that requires a turn—and we talk about that turn after the song is over (see Appendix A for other examples).

Adults are encouraged to talk about, measure, and record children's height and measure lengths of things using hands and feet. There is little research to show the effects of such tasks on preschoolers' subsequent mathematics achievement. Given what we know about adult engagement in visual spatial talk and activities, one would suspect that doing these sorts of activities with young children would be helpful.

COMPARISON

Comparison tasks include activities that require children to compare quantities for differences or sameness. Activities that compare quantities for differences focus on the ideas of *more* and *less*. Activities that compare quantities for sameness focus on the ideas of *parity* or *equality*.

To recap, young children have been found to be able to compare numbers and recognize changes in representations of numbers relatively early in life—by about 1 week of age (Starkey, 1992; Starkey, Spelke, & Gelman, 1983; 1990). By about 4 months of age, young children notice differences when, for example, there is a change from one dot to two dots on a screen (Starkey & Cooper, 1980). Initially, infants can only discriminate between one and two objects, but by about 10 months of age, their ability to discriminate between larger numbers seems to be well established, even in conditions where sounds are matched with the stimuli (e.g., numbers of sounds match the number of objects; Lipton & Spelke, 2004) and in additive conditions (e.g., adding five more dots to an image; McCrink & Wynn, 2004). The ability to discriminate between nonsymbolic representations of numbers (e.g., four dots to represent the number four) and symbolic representations of numbers (e.g., the number symbol "4") develops as the child ages.

Research clearly shows that very young children, even before talking, have the ability to discriminate between numbers (Xu & Spelke, 2000). There has been some debate, however, on exactly how this happens in the infant mind. Some propose that there is an inborn part in the brain that notices the changes in quantity (Meck & Church, 1983). Others propose that the child is noticing a change in the overall spatial representation (e.g., that it is taking up more space visually)—particularly for sets of objects smaller than four. The brain has a process that tracks information about objects by their location and shape (Kahneman, Treisman, & Gibbs, 1992). It is likely a combination of both of these neural mechanisms that allows humans to develop this sensitivity to numbers and changes in magnitude.

The ability to compare quantities in both symbolic (e.g., numerals) and nonsymbolic forms (e.g., dots) of numbers has been correlated with children's performance on a standardized test of mathematical ability at as early as 3 years of age (Mazzocco, Feigenson, & Halberda, 2011; Nosworthy, 2013). Coupled with the evidence that young children have the ability to recognize changes in magnitude and that such ability is related to early mathematical ability, adults should include developmentally appropriate opportunities for young children to engage in comparison-type tasks that include comparing quantities of more or less and comparing quantities that are equal. Text Box 5.2 lists a couple of comparison tasks from our workshop.

There are a couple of findings about magnitude comparison from cognitive science worth knowing for those supporting young children. First, the *numeric distance effect* suggests that numbers that have a greater numerical distance between them make it easier for individuals to tell which is smaller or larger (Brannon, 2002; Holloway & Ansari, 2008; Xu & Spelke, 2000). For example, most of us will find it much easier and faster to tell that a group of 10 objects is larger than a group of 2 objects than it is to tell that a group of 5 objects is bigger than a group of 4. Second, researchers have found that there is a directional effect involving the association of numbers with spatial left–right response coordinates called the *spatial–numerical association of response codes* (SNARC) effect (Dehaene, Bossini, & Giraux, 1993). The SNARC effect indicates that numbers are organized in the brain with the smallest starting on the left and then progressing to larger numbers moving right. These findings support the belief that humans have internal number line representations such as the one shown in Figure 5.4.

Some cultural differences, however, have been found in children who learn to read from right to left, such as, for example, children who learn to read in Arabic. Preschoolers who are described as preliterate—that is, who cannot yet read—only exhibit the SNARC effect with nonsymbolic representations of numbers (e.g., dots or objects) and with sets smaller than four (Patro & Haman, 2012). This should be kept in mind as a developmentally appropriate benchmark when engaging in comparison tasks. Likewise, it is important to remember that children may have individual differences in their abilities to perform these tasks.

ADDING AND SUBTRACTING

Adding and subtracting are familiar concepts for most adults. It may surprise you to know, however, that very young children are also able to engage in simple addition and subtraction (McCrink & Wynn, 2004). For young children, adding involves combining two positive numbers (known as "addends") together to form a larger positive number. Subtracting involves taking a larger positive number and subtracting a smaller value so that there is a remainder.

Children often first learn about *zero* during informal everyday addition and subtraction tasks (e.g., "You have eaten your cookies! There are none left"). Typically, *zero* is understood by children as *nothing*. The addition or subtraction of zero is considered a relatively straightforward concept that young children can grasp easily (Clements & Sarama, 2009, p. 22). Though understanding the concept of *zero* is straightforward, we should hold off introducing the numeral "0" to young children before they understand the five counting principles. The mapping of the concept of *nothing* to a numeral "0" that represents something may be a bit confusing to the little ones.

Research about infants adding and subtracting has produced some conflicting evidence as to exactly when infants develop these abilities and the mechanisms that contribute to their development (Bisanz, Sherman, Rasmussen, & Ho, 2005). Some research has found evidence of early addition and subtraction skills at about 4–5 months old (Wynn, 1992a). Other researchers suggest that the evidence does not necessarily mean that infants are processing numerical data, but rather that they are processing other, nonnumerical data in the form of tracking objects, as we discussed earlier (Mix, Huttenlocher, & Levine, 2002).

Regardless of the debate regarding addition and subtraction in infancy, there is consensus among researchers that young children by the age of 3 are capable of adding and subtracting up to the number 5 (Cross et al., 2009, p. 130; Fuson & Willis, 1988). By the age of 4, children can add and subtract up to the number 8, and by the age of 5 they can add and subtract up to the number 10 (Cross et al., 2009, p. 130).

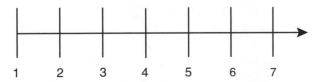

Figure 5.4. Number line.

||||||| TEXT BOX 5.2.   FIGURES COMPARISON ACTIVITIES

More or less?

For this game, we use a variety of counting objects such as chain links, cubes, figurines, and balls. We first start by creating two very distinctly different piles, and then we ask the children which one has more or less. A good strategy is to the model the solution: "Does this one have more or less? Yes, this one has more!"

Next, we make smaller, more manageable counting sets. "Which one has more? Let's count them! One, two. Two. That pile has two. One. This pile has one. This pile has more. There are two!"

Go fish!

For this game, we put two fish—although you can use any objects—in our lunch bag–sized bags that we refer to as "magic bags." We then have the children remove the fish and count them as they remove them. "How many fishes are in this magic bag? One, two. There are two! How many in this bag? One, two? There are two. There are the same numbers of fish in each bag. Two here and two in this bag."

Children under the age of 3 seem to do better with addition and subtraction problems that are presented without much use of language (i.e., nonverbal; Fuson, 1988; Levine, Jordan, & Huttenlocher, 1992). In nonverbal problems, objects are used to model addition and subtraction and children are asked to model the solution (Jordan, Huttenlocher, & Levine, 1992). So, for example, children are shown four balls. The balls are then covered, and two balls are taken away. The child is then asked to model the same mathematical situation with his or her own balls—indicating an understanding of subtraction or addition. The task is seen as nonverbal because no language use is required by the child. Another example of a nonverbal addition or subtraction task is a block game for which children add or subtract colored blocks in rows to make each of the rows equal (Krasa & Shunkwiler, 2009, p. 67).

As children get older, they become better at answering questions that are verbally presented and then learn to answer hypothetical or scenario-based questions (also commonly known as *real-life contexts*; Huttenlocher, Jordan, & Levine, 1994). However, the hypothetical or scenario-based format seems to be the most challenging, even for 5-year-olds (Levine et al., 1992). It is interesting to note that the use of hypothetical or scenario-based question formats is highly endorsed in school-based mathematics, with some suggesting such real-world formats are easier for children to relate to and understand.

Young children have been found to use a variety of strategies to add and subtract, and as might be anticipated, counting ability is vital for addition and subtraction (Geary & Hoard, 2005, p. 258). Early adding and subtracting strategies include the use of fingers and/or objects and often involve the counting of all given objects. However, as Starkey and Gelman (1982) describe, when young children are presented with small numbers in addition and subtraction tasks, sometimes overt counting strategies (e.g., counting on fingers) are not used. As the children progress developmentally, they then learn to add by counting up either from the larger of the two numbers being added (known as the "min" strategy) or from the smaller of the two numbers being added (known as the "max" strategy; Kamii, 2000).

Subtraction is slightly different. Fuson and Willis (1988) describe how some children "subtract up" by starting with the smaller number and then counting to the large number. So five minus three would be counted as "three, four, five," with an answer of two, because two digits separate three and five in the counting sequence. With smaller sets of numbers less than four, children can subitize (i.e., knowing the quantity without physically having to count the items in a set) for the solution. As they mature, young children have also been observed to use mental representations (in their head) to solve simple addition and subtraction problems.

Children who do better in nonsymbolic (i.e., objects versus number symbols) addition and subtraction at the beginning of formal schooling have been found to do better on tests of mathematics achievement at the end of kindergarten. This shows that their mathematical experiences and development in addition and subtraction prior to formal schooling have important implications for academic outcomes at least 1 year later (Gilmore, McCarthy, & Spelke, 2010). Nonsymbolic addition and subtraction skills may in fact have lasting implications for mathematics achievement well beyond kindergarten. In research studying the nonverbal approximation abilities (i.e., judging images of objects and assessing more or less between pairs of images) of 14-year-olds, achievement was significantly correlated with children's standardized mathematics scores from kindergarten (Halberda, Mazzocco, & Feigenson, 2008). These results again highlight the importance of the early childhood years prior to formal schooling.

During LittleCounters, we play games that encourage addition and subtraction while connecting the task closely to one or more of the counting strategies. For example, one of the games we play is "Scarf toss" (Figure 5.5).

Young children have incredible fun with these scarves. That being said, any object safe for throwing in the air can be used for this game. The scarves, which are light, colorful, and translucent, are tossed between the adults and the children, billowing up through the air before they come to rest near the child or even on the child. The game plays out like this:

Figure 5.5.   Scarf tossing game.

Adult: Get ready! Here we go! One! *(tossing the scarf and showing one finger)* Good catch! How many do you have?

Child: One!

Adult: I am going to throw another one. You have one and I am going to throw another one. How many will you have? One, two. *(modeling with fingers and then tossing the scarf)* Good catch! How many do you have?

Child: One, two. Two!

Adult: Great job!

Adult: Okay, throw one back. How many do you have now?

Child: One!

Adult: Good job! Yes, you had two and you threw one back so you have one left! *(showing two fingers and then putting one finger down)*

PATTERNING AND EARLY ALGEBRA

Counting words are among the very first patterns young children learn, and this is known as the *stable order principle*, described in Chapter 3. Patterning is, according to Clements and Sarama (2009), *"a search for mathematical regularities and structures"* (author's emphasis; p. 190). Constructing patterns and identifying patterns are common activities among young children (Seo & Ginsburg, 2004), where the complexity and the predictability of patterns increase as the child ages (Klein, 2004). Young children can be observed constructing simple patterns with toys and everyday objects in simple formats of ABAB, in which A is one element or object and B is another object (e.g., two red blocks, two green blocks, two red blocks, two green blocks). Young children, although demonstrating an ability to construct such simple patterns, tend to be prone to mistakes in their patterning up to the start of formal schooling or age 5 (Klein, 2004).

Algebra, in very simple terms, involves discovering the value of some missing or unknown amount. How then are patterning and algebra related? According to Clements and Sarama (2009, p. 52), "algebra begins with a search of patterns." By asking young children to identify and describe patterns, they learn to generalize. For example, simple games predicting the number of blocks in a pattern if a particular pattern continues would require such generalization on behalf of the child. The child would have to complete the patterning task and determine the unknown quantity of the final pattern. Asking young children to describe patterns and then raising "what if" types of questions can inspire such generalizations. When in school, young children are often asked to describe the pattern rule, and much later in elementary education, they are asked to define the "general term" (i.e., describe the pattern algebraically using both letters for unknown variables and numbers).

According to Erna Yackel (1997), early algebraic reasoning can be "accomplished through activities that encourage children to move beyond numerical reasoning to more general reasoning about relationships, quantity, and ways of notating and symbolizing" (p. 280). An example would be those scenarios that ask a child to think about the relationship between more and less: "Mommy has two more apples; how many apples does mommy have?" The unknown quantity is an example of early algebra—without the symbols! The symbolic representations of this addition problem come after the start of formal schooling.

Surprisingly, very little research actually exists related to early algebraic reasoning (Moomaw, 2011, p. 73), yet the importance of algebraic reasoning has been nevertheless recognized in many policy statements, such as that of the National Council of Teachers of Mathematics (NCTM; 2000). Some evidence exists to suggest that children from more advantaged backgrounds experience more patterning and early algebra prior to schooling and thus do better at it than those children from less advantaged backgrounds (Klein, 2004).

Here are some examples of questions that can inspire patterning and early algebra:

- If there was another button, what color would it be?

- How many times does the clock chime? How many chimes will there be next?

- If I have n more, how many do I have?

- If I give you n, how many do I have left?

- If every week our puppy grows by one hand, how many hands long will he be in 2 more weeks?

ESTIMATION

Estimation involves approximating a quantity. The approximation can be either very good, sometimes known as an "educated guess," or very far off. Researchers Robert Siegler and Julie Booth (2005) define estimation as a "process of translating between alternatively quantitative representations, at least one of which is an inexact" (p. 198). In other words, it is comparing two quantities in which one of the quantities is not exact (e.g., comparing two blocks to a pile of blocks that is not easily countable). Quantitative representations can be either symbolic (e.g., numbers) or nonsymbolic (e.g., objects).

Siegler and Booth (2005) suggest that when it comes to estimation, many school-age children and adults "are surprisingly bad" (p. 197). This seems like a reasonable assertion. Most people have played the "How many jelly beans in the jar?" estimation game and are often completely surprised at the amount actually in the jar when the count is revealed. According to Siegler and Booth, estimation is challenging because of the complex processes involved. Estimation involves a multifaceted interaction among several mathematical concepts and processes, including counting, adding, subtracting, comparing, and/or measuring. To add to the complexity, there is no one right answer to an estimation problem—only better or more accurate estimations!

Young children have been known to be particularly illogical when it comes to tasks of estimation, sometimes even giving their age when asked to estimate (Moomaw, 2011, p. 151; Moomaw & Heronymus, 1995). As with most skills, a person's ability to estimate gets better with age, as the strategies used for estimation become more elegant and move beyond simply guessing (Matsuda & Matsuda, 1983; Newman & Berger, 1984). In the "guess the number of jellybeans" type of task, children may try to count or use some form of addition and, later, multiplication strategy. Like geometry, estimation has also been found to be malleable in that young children's ability to estimate improves over time with instruction (Matsuda & Matsuda, 1987) and practice (Powel, Morelli, & Nusbaum, 1994).

Much of the research related to estimation focuses on a young child's ability to locate the proximity of a number on a number line. For example, a child might be asked to indicate where the number four would be positioned on a number line that spanned from one to five. When children position the number four close to the number five, they are seen as having better estimation skills, and hence understanding of numbers, than if they placed it close to the number one or even the middle of the range.

Although there is evidence to suggest a child's estimation ability is related to his or her mathematical ability at age 5 (Booth & Siegler, 2006), the evidence suggesting that estimation plays a role in improving mathematical ability over time is questionable (Muldoon, Towse, Simms, Perra, & Menzies, 2013). Not surprisingly, an understanding of numbers, including counting ability, has been found to be a key factor in improving estimation as well as mathematics achievement (Berteletti, Lucangeli, Piazza, Dehaene, & Zorzi, 2010; Muldoon et al., 2013).

In addition to supporting the ongoing development of counting before children start school, adults can support young children's development of estimation skills through activities that allow for the following:

- Providing opportunities for repeated estimation (i.e., guessing)

- Modeling of strategies by the adult (e.g., "I added all the bottom row and then added two more ..."), even encouraging counting as an important strategy

- Guessing using small quantities to begin with (less than four objects) so the child can begin to develop confidence with marked success through simply subitizing for the answer (i.e., knowing the number of objects in a set without actually counting them)

- Making the estimation task fun and game-like

Make guessing and estimation part of the everyday interactions in your environment. Choose different objects to include in a guessing jar, paying close attention to developmentally appropriate quantities (e.g., do not ask a 3-year-old to guess a jar of 1,000 objects). Objects could be food (e.g., apples, oranges, potatoes), household objects (e.g., spoons, buttons, mittens), or toys (e.g., blocks, figurines, small counting toys). No research studies are known that examine this sort of approach to learning estimation during early childhood; however, we would wager that it will likely improve estimation skills.

PROPORTIONAL REASONING

Proportional reasoning involves understanding fractions and thus requires an understanding of the parts that make up a whole quantity (e.g., two halves make a whole). Young children and adults often jointly engage in proportional reasoning all the time—although it is perhaps not recognized as proportional reasoning. Sharing of food, toys, and space all require proportional reasoning. Sharing halves of an apple or orange is commonplace during snack time for young children.

Research suggests that by about age 3, young children have an emergent understanding of proportions and are able to compare and match fractions when comparing parts (e.g., half an orange and half a box of chocolates both represent half of a quantity; Mix, Levine, & Huttenlocher, 1999; Singer-Freeman & Goswami, 2001). The fraction of *half* is particularly important to young children's proportional reasoning and is viewed as a benchmark for their emergent understanding (Singer-Freeman & Goswami, 2001; Spinillo & Bryant, 1991; 1999). Young children's basic understanding of proportion is intuitive and develops without any formal instruction (Spinillo & Bryant, 1999). Reasoning about relationships *between* parts and a whole, however, happens only after the beginning of formal schooling (Sophian & Wood, 1997).

No direct studies were found that report implications of proportional reasoning in preschool children for later mathematics achievement. However, Byrnes and Wasik (2009) included proportional reasoning in their comprehensive study of factors influencing academic achievement of kindergartners during their first 3 years of schooling. Children's success was highly influenced in this study, as in others we have already discussed, by the mathematics they had learned before school.

Hunting (2003) used a story context to examine 3-year-olds' proportional reasoning; young children used visualization (creation of a mental model in the mind) as a primary thinking tool for evaluating proportions. Hunting also found that children used visualization to evaluate proportions even when they were not presented with physical stimuli. Children also used "finger" sets to represent proportions from within the story. These results suggest that counting could also be an important precursor to developing proportional reasoning.

Sharing, in particular sharing among children in everyday and routine activities, provides an ideal context for both introducing fractions and using the language of proportional reasoning. For example, you could preface the sharing of blocks between two children by saying "half for each of you." Food is another ideal example, and working with shapes in activities that involve putting together or dividing objects can also be a great opportunity for injecting proportion play into everyday activities.

PROBLEM SOLVING

In early childhood, a child's ability to problem-solve is closely related to changes in brain development that happen around the age of 3 (Welsh, Friedman, & Spieker, 2006; Zero to Three, 2009). This may explain why younger children problem-solve best with nonverbal problems (i.e., using objects and modeling with the objects) and problems that do not involve situations proposed to model real life (see earlier section on addition and subtraction; Huttenlocher et al., 1994).

Problem solving in early childhood looks different from problem solving in elementary school. The types of mathematical problem solving children engage in prior to formal schooling mostly emerge out of play, involve concrete objects, and may or may not involve other children or adults (Charlesworth & Leali, 2012). The main means of understanding a child's problem solving is through observation and engagement with the child (Piccolo & Test, 2011).

Young children use a variety of strategies for problem solving, including 1) watching or working with another child or other children (Tarim, 2009), 2) engaging an adult, 3) trial and error, and 4) planning (Shiakalli & Zacharos, 2012). As might be anticipated, young children's understanding of number words has been found to be important for problem solving (Patel & Canobi, 2010). Adults can use a variety of strategies to support and promote problem solving, such as asking "what if" types of questions and formulating challenges that are doable but still advance a child's understanding.

ORDINAL NUMBERS

According to Clements and Sarama (2009), ordinal numbers are those that "involv[e] the words 'first, second . . .' [to] indicate the position in a series or ordering" (p. 45). The authors go on to explain that these ordinal numbers represent a location in a series of events, tasks, or objects they are describing.

Although children typically start learning about ordinal numbers after the start of formal schooling around age 6 (Fuson, 1988), younger children actually begin to understand ordinal numbers by about age 3 or 4 (Clements & Sarama, 2009; Colomé & Noël, 2012; Cross et al., 2009, p. 167). However, some studies report that children up to 5 years old still make high levels of errors in ordinal number use (Fischer & Beckey, 1990). The most frequent error among young children is generalizing the ending of the ordinal number across all other ordinal numbers by affixing "-th" or "-st" onto the count words (e.g., one-th, two-th). This type of error may not be as problematic in some languages because of the structure of the number words in different languages (Miller, Major, Shu,

& Zhang, 2000). It seems, however, that using ordinal numbers is a concept that follows the development of a sound understanding of cardinality (Colomé & Noël, 2012).

Ordinal numbers are very relevant to any "first this, then that" task you might engage in with young children. Surprisingly, many parents tell us that they had never thought of rewording "first this, then that" tasks to use ordinal words. For example, a parent may say, "First we'll tidy up; then we'll have snack." An alternate approach would be to use ordinal numbers and say, "First we'll tidy up; second we'll have snack." Parents who have participated in LittleCounters share with us that increased use of ordinal numbers is one of the most noticeable changes in their use of mathematical talk in the home. During our LittleCounters sessions, we transition between the activities using precisely this approach.

Although we play various games to model ordinal numbers, our main way of focusing on ordinal numbers is through stories. Inspired by a true story of ducks at sea, children's author Eric Carle (2005) has written a book that describes the adventures of the ducks using ordinal numbers. He shares with his readers descriptions of each duck, from the "1st" duck through to the "10th" duck. The story is charming and provides a unique and original contribution to the plethora of counting books available.

CHAPTER SUMMARY

Counting and an understanding of numbers are central to all the other mathematical thinking we describe in this chapter. Our intention in this chapter was to illustrate that 1) young children can engage in various types of mathematics prior to formal schooling and 2) engagement with these other types of mathematical thinking has been shown to facilitate mathematical thinking with important implications for mathematics achievement after the start of formal schooling. Much of the research focuses on specific forms of mathematical thinking in relation to mathematics achievement, largely because it is hard to separate out the multiple factors that contribute to mathematical thinking and performance.

In reading the summaries of the different types of mathematical thinking in this chapter, it should be clear that there are connections between them. All these forms of mathematical thinking require an understanding of counting and numbers. Geometry links measurement and counting. Estimation, comparison, and counting are also intertwined. Ordinal numbers are crucial to adding and subtracting, and understanding ordinals is dependent on a sound understanding of counting. Measurement links counting, ordinal numbers, and additive and subtractive reasoning. Proportional reasoning requires an understanding of measurement, counting, and geometry. Problem solving is often the context for all these mathematical tasks. Our point is that there are many concepts and skills in mathematics that are interwoven. The key is for adults to help young children make those connections prior to entering formal schooling, because children are ready for them earlier than you might think. They are born LittleCounters.

Chapter 6

Mathematics in Everyday Routines and Activities

Adults often use a "first this, then that" approach to assisting young children in organizing their time in daily routines. For example, you may have said to your child, "First we'll clean up our toys; then we'll have a snack." This "first this, then that" approach, coupled with some minor changes in the language we use, can be a way of teaching children about ordinal numbers—the count position of an item, task, or object. How? Instead of "first this, then that," consider using "first this, second that, third …" Use your fingers as you are ordering the tasks using these ordinal words, and you have created a learning moment out of an everyday and routine organizational task such as cleaning up.

Infusing numbers and mathematical concepts in everyday activities is important in early mathematics learning. Yet doing this is also a challenge for many of us, due to the hectic nature of taking care of little ones either at home or in a child care setting. The National Association for the Education of Young Children (NAEYC) and the National Council of Teachers of Mathematics (NCTM; 2002) joint position statement on early mathematics education endorses the inclusion of mathematics in everyday activities of young children, recognizing the compelling evidence that it affects children's academic outcomes once they start school. Children who come to school understanding the basic counting principles outlined in Chapter 3 and, to some extent, those mathematical ideas outlined in Chapter 5 do better in mathematics and other subjects. This head start advantage they have is also often sustained throughout their schooling (Burchinal et al., 2008; Duncan et al., 2007; Geary, Hoard, Nugent, & Bailey, 2013; La Paro & Pianta, 2000; Romano, Babchishin, Pagani, & Kohen, 2010). There is an undeniable advantage for a young child who comes to school with an understanding of numbers and simple mathematical concepts—similar to the advantage that many of us associate with reading skills. Unfortunately, education has not been shown to consistently close this gap between those children who come ready to learn mathematics and those who do not.

A child's early understanding of the counting principles has some amazing implications for his or her future learning. This is *particularly* remarkable given how easy it can be for adults to build in more opportunities to engage with numbers in relatively straightforward, simple, and natural ways. The mathematics we are discussing (e.g., counting, adding, subtracting, comparing, patterning, shape identification) is easy and accessible for most people, and that is good news for those of us who are apprehensive or even fearful when it comes to mathematics.

Informal, everyday activities are great opportunities for children to learn about numbers. Research has shown that routine mathematical tasks such as board and card games, shopping, or cooking were more predictive of children's performance using a standardized test of early mathematical ability (Blevins-Knabe & Musun-Miller, 1996; LeFevre et al., 2009; Skwarchuk, 2009) than merely teaching children to recognize numerals. Moreover, LeFevre and her colleagues (2009) report that the impact of these informal and everyday activities on mathematics ability was consistent with research relating home literacy experiences to children's vocabulary.

It is reasonable for us to expect children to come to school knowing about numbers and some mathematical concepts. Research has shown us that children are clearly capable of doing more mathematics than we think (Ginsburg, Cannon, Eisenband, & Pappas, 2006; Seo & Ginsburg, 2004). Consequently, in this chapter, we focus on illustrating 1) how numbers and mathematics both exist naturally in the everyday routines and activities of young children and 2) how numbers and mathematics can be purposefully infused easily and often into these routines and activities.

Both the counting principles we covered in Chapter 3 and the identification of symbolic representations of numbers can be included in everyday activities. For example, the abstraction principle (the idea that anything and everything can be counted) is especially reinforced when counting becomes an everyday part of tasks, using different objects and even ideas. Children can learn to identify numbers through tasks as simple as reading numbers from signs or their home address. The stable order principle (counting numbers in the right sequence) is reinforced when it is repeated over and over again across a variety of counting objects, tasks, and ideas. When children understand these first two counting principles, they have a strong base for learning the one-to-one correspondence (counting objects only once) and the cardinality (total of the set) principles.

The majority of young children are cared for in homes by relatives or immediate family. Only approximately 30% to 40% of young children are cared for in child care settings (Barnett, 2013; National Center for Education Statistics, 2005). Studies of these early child care settings indicate that almost 40% of a child's time is spent on routines (Winton & Buysse, 2005). Routines include dressing, eating, doing or assisting with chores (e.g., putting away toys), grooming (e.g., brushing teeth, washing hands), and helping in the kitchen (e.g., setting the table, clearing the dishes). Similar approximations of time spent on routines are seen in children in home-care settings. Consequently, everyday routines can provide important opportunities for learning.

Whether engaging in routines or other structured or semistructured learning tasks, recent large-scale studies of preschool settings in the United States have found that young children spend only approximately 6% of their time in total on activities with either a primary or supplementary focus on mathematics (Early et al., 2005; Winton & Buysse, 2005). Studies of activities in the home, child care, or early childhood education setting show similarly low levels of engagement with numbers and mathematical concepts (e.g., Tudge & Doucet, 2004). Not surprisingly, at home, families tend to focus more on literacy development and less on numeracy development (Cannon & Ginsburg, 2008; Tudge & Doucet, 2004). In fact, numeracy development represented the lowest amount of time of all the content-based areas of early learning (literacy, science, art). This might be due to the fact that studies have shown that 1) early childhood educators (ECEs) are underprepared in the area of early mathematical learning and 2) appropriate professional development for ECEs in early mathematical cognition and pedagogy is scarce (Bowman, Donovan, & Burns, 2000; Clements & Sarama, 2009; Cross, Woods, & Schweingruber, 2009).

Despite the many empirical studies that have demonstrated that young children are cognitively capable of engaging in activities geared toward developing mathematical abilities from a very young age, mathematical learning is not a consistent focus of education in the early years (Andersson, 2007; Butterworth, 1999a, 1999b; Clements, 1999; Clements & Sarama, 2009; Ginsburg & Baroody, 2003; Ginsburg, Lee, & Boyd, 2008; Sarama & Clements, 2009; 2006; Wynn, 1990). From our own experience working with parents, caregivers, and ECEs, adults recognize the importance of mathematics in early childhood but report not fully understanding how to infuse mathematical concepts and ideas into their interactions with children.

Some research also suggests that some adults consider mathematics learning to be unimportant in the early years, even though there is compelling research to the contrary (Blevins-Knabe, Austin, Musun, Eddy, & Jones, 2000; Cannon & Ginsburg, 2008). Understandably, literacy is more of a focus and perhaps an easier focus for adults (Barbarin et al., 2008). Let us not forget that it took more than 20 years for researchers, educators, not-for-profit organizations, libraries, and policy makers to bring early literacy to the forefront at this point.

A simple Internet search will reveal long lists of free literacy programs and countless "how to" lists for young children and even infants! For example, the Dolly Parton Imagination Library program offers free books to young children in the United States, Canada, and the United Kingdom. In Canada, many local libraries and hospitals provide free baby book packages to parents of newborns and young children. One such program, called the "Welcome Baby Package," is offered by the Edmonton Public Libraries in Calgary. Similarly, in the United Kingdom, a "BookStart Baby" pack is offered to parents with infants during their first year through their health professionals or libraries.

On the other hand, if you were to do an Internet search for early mathematics programs for infants and toddlers, you might find articles on why teaching mathematics to young kids is important and a few tips on how to engage in mathematical activities. However, it is difficult to find early mathematics programs similar to the early literacy programs. Perhaps this is one of the main reasons why our LittleCounters workshop has been so well received by parents, caregivers, and ECEs. Our LittleCounters workshop and this book are our attempt to contribute to the shift to an increased focus on mathematics learning right from the beginning of a newborn's life.

Unfortunately, many adults also have to deal with residual negative feelings about mathematics from their own experiences with the subject matter. More people fear numbers and mathematics than any other subject area. Adults have been known to describe themselves as "disabled" or "afraid" when it comes to mathematics. Yet less than 6% of people actually suffer from the mathematics learning challenge known as dyscalculia (Butterworth, 1999a, 1999b; Dehaene, Molko, Cohen, & Wilson, 2004). This means that approximately 94% of people *are* able to do very complex mathematics with the appropriate environmental opportunities.

The NAEYC and NCTM (2002) joint position statement on early mathematics learning emphasizes the importance of adults being positive about mathematics learning. Research has shown that preschoolers' numeracy scores were predicted by their adult caregivers' positive reports of personal experience with mathematics (Skwarchuk, 2009). Adults who have had less than positive experiences *can* change their outlook on mathematics. Adults routinely set aside their own biases when they recognize the benefits for a young child. For example, adults routinely emphasize the need for a balanced and healthy diet with children despite perhaps not eating healthy themselves!

Adults need to set aside their own biases and previous bad experiences with mathematics so that they are not unwittingly mapped onto a child's emerging affective feelings toward numbers, mathematics, and their ability to engage with these concepts. This is definitely easier said than done. However, it is our hope that our readers are able to overcome their own apprehension toward mathematics by breaking down the barrier of viewing mathematics as boring and challenging. Most, if not all, of our LittleCounters workshop participants have shown us that our goal is attainable.

To recap, the mathematics we are talking about includes the counting principles outlined in Chapter 3 and those concepts in Chapter 5—the identification of symbolic representations of numbers, simple addition and subtraction, measurement, shape identification, some basic geometry, and proportional reasoning (simple fractions and percentages). This is mathematics that most of us can do without much effort with some level of intentionality. In the following sections, we give some more examples of how mathematics can be easily incorporated into a child's everyday activities.

The ideas we present have four key underlying components: 1) interaction between a child and an adult; 2) an awareness and willingness to see mathematics, especially numbers, everywhere; 3) a sensitivity to a child's actions and developmental progression (Guralnick, 2006); and 4) a purposeful approach to engaging in the mathematization of everyday routines. Remember to use the "Name It, Show It (and Say It), Touch It (and Say It), Move It (and Say It), Say It" strategy to facilitate the mathematical learning process.

MEALS

Children love to be in the kitchen helping out, making a mess, or eating. The opportunities during mealtimes for children to engage in counting, measurement, shape recognition, estimation, comparison tasks, and other mathematical tasks are plentiful.

Preparing Food

Very young children (under age 2) do not typically help with preparing food. However, starting at age 2, young children are curious and eager to be involved in the food preparation activities. Often children help with baking or preparing simple parts of meals. They want to help, but they also are motivated to eat!

Preparing food might require a different approach when including children. For example, measuring quantities in cups is usually done one cup at a time with one cup for each ingredient. When working with young children, for example, in baking, you might consider measuring out at least one ingredient using three different containers. This allows you to 1) count the cups (one-to-one correspondence); 2) ask "How many?" after they have counted the cups of flour (cardinality); and 3) ask "If we count from left to right, do we still get the same number of cups of flour?" (order irrelevance). Text Box 6.1 provides an example of the kinds of questions and interactions that could be used when cooking with children. Note that an *error correction strategy* is used in this example as a learning tool. An error correction strategy is one in which the adult makes the mistake and then demonstrates the correction in order to illustrate an idea or create an opportunity for learning.

Setting the Table

It is very common to have young children help set the table for meals. Counting can easily be incorporated into setting the table by counting plates, forks, spoons, bowls, and so forth. Chairs and place mats can also be counted (Figure 6.1). The key is to be sure to show the numbers with your hands as you count, asking the child to also show you how many. The other key is to

---

| | | | | | | | **TEXT BOX 6.1.   COUNTING INGREDIENTS** |

Adult:	Do you want to help me measure the flour for the cookies?
Child:	Yes!
Adult:	We need three cups of flour. Can you count to three?
Child:	One, two, three!
Adult:	Excellent. You counted to three. *(Adult holds up three fingers.)*
Adult:	We need three cups to measure the flour because we need three cups for our cookies. Let's get our cups out! *(Cups are lined up on the counter, and one extra cup is included.)*
Adult:	We need three cups. Do we have three cups? Let's count to make sure.
Child:	One, two, three. *(Adult helps by moving the cups over across the counter, showing that there is one extra cup.)*
Adult:	Oh, my. We have one extra cup. We'll put that one away. Now we have three. *(Adult now counts the cups again, moving them back across the counter using his or her fingers to show the numbers and then reinforces cardinality by repeating the number three.)*

Once the cookies are baked fresh from the oven, the adult and child can then count how many cookies there are and divide them equally between themselves or others. We could even extend this baking activity to an afternoon tea party for two or three.

Figure 6.1. Setting the table.

reinforce cardinality by always asking "How many?" after the child finishes counting the objects. It is also an excellent daily routine to instill the one-to-one correspondence principle, because it is a concrete example a young child can use to map one person to one place setting of plate, utensils, and place mat. Children who do not understand the cardinality concept will answer with a random number, sometimes their own age or the next number in the counting sequence, when asked to give the total quantity in a set. Conversation starters around setting the table could include the following:

· What shape is the dinner plate?

· How many colors are on the place mat/dinner plate?

· How many plates do we need? How many people in our family?

· Do we have enough spoons? We need four.

· Grandma is coming to dinner tonight, so we'll need an extra plate at the table. Usually we have four plates, but we'll need one more. How many plates will we need?

A fun arts and crafts activity that is related to the theme of setting tables that you and your child could do together is making your own plates or place mats. You could ask the child to draw or paint objects or animals such as bumblebees on paper plates or place mats. Alternatively, painted hand-prints on a placement are also fun and are particularly useful in highlighting the one-to-one correspondence of our physical fingers and the fingerprints on the plate or place mat. Keep in mind the five counting principles—one-to-one correspondence, stable order, cardinality, abstraction, and order irrelevance—while having fun creating art!

Eating

Young children either love to eat or are fussy eaters. Although there are mixed reports on the appropriateness of making mealtime a game or fun, food is probably one of the easiest objects to use to help teach and practice the counting principles. Again, the key is to remember "Name It, Show It (and Say It), Touch It (and Say It), Move It (and Say It), Say It." For fussy eaters, making a game of the meal may help. Counting while the food is on the plate is one option, but another option is counting during the serving of the food items. The child can join in the counting and can practice the stable order principle (e.g., one before two, two before three) at the same time. While the food is on the plate, engaging in conversations about *more* or *less* can be fun. The key to exploring parity (same) or magnitude (more or less) with young children is to keep the proportions either different enough that the child can make the judgment just by looking or small enough that quantities either are countable within the child's developmentally appropriate range or can be subitized (i.e., knowing the quantity without counting). Here are some conversation starters related to food:

· Do we have the same number of baby potatoes on our plate?

· Are there more blueberries on your plate or in the bowl?

· Mom just ate one spoonful of squash. Are you going to have one too?

· How many bowls of snacks do we have on the table? Let's see what snacks we have and count how many bowls we have.

Cleaning Up the Kitchen

Children can learn to help clean up after meals and cooking from a very young age. They can assist with things such as wiping down surfaces, putting utensils away, and bringing dishes into the kitchen after a meal. Here are some conversation starters with an emphasis on ordinal numbers in cleanup tasks:

· First, can you please bring your plate? Second, please bring me your place mat. *(showing one and then two fingers)*

· Can you help me first bring the ketchup to the kitchen? Second, we'll bring in the plates, and then finally, third, we'll wipe down the table! *(showing one, two, then three fingers)*

If the child is too young to do some of these activities safely, try letting the child watch you put away and wash the pots and dishes in soapy water. Alternatively, the child could be given a container with some dish soap and some plastic dishes and utensils to mimic the washing activity in perhaps a minikitchen center (Figure 6.2).

BEDTIME

Bedtime is another ideal time to think about ways to infuse counting and numbers. The following sections outline some of the main tasks in the bedtime routine. The order of the tasks varies from family to family and perhaps even between cultures. "First this, second that" is a good strategy for including ordinal numbers in the organization of bedtime routines.

Reading Stories

The most ideal way to incorporate mathematics in the bedtime reading routine is through stories about counting, shapes, mathematics, and so forth. A rich collection of counting books is available for young children. Some of these are listed in Appendix A. Key things to watch for in books about numbers for young children are features on pages that allow for opportunities for children to engage in one-to-one correspondence. We typically recommend books that count forward for children under age 5. In our picture counting books, *LittleCounters® at the Market* (Lee & Kotsopoulos, 2012) and *LittleCounters® around the World Count* (Kotsopoulos & Lee, in press), we also show images of hands to help with the *show it* aspect of our "Name It, Show It (and Say It), Touch It (and Say It), Move It (and Say It), Say It" strategy for supporting young learners. Also included in our books are number lines with dots corresponding to the count number to show the relationship among numbers, especially the ordinality of numbers.

Figure 6.2. Minikitchen center.

Different books have different features that may not necessarily support number learning. Here are some examples of text features that may not be useful for young children learning to count:

· Books that count by 2, 5, or 10

· Books that count beyond 10 (for younger children)

· Images that are complex and make one-to-one correspondence challenging

· Books that count backward

· Books with more complex mathematics such as adding, subtracting, or fractions

Attend to book features carefully. Of course, stories read to young children do not need to be restricted to stories that are specifically about mathematics. For example, a story about a young boy searching for his missing pet frog through a forest could also be used to introduce mathematical talk by identifying and counting the number of animals he meets along the way (Frog, where are you?; Mercer, 1969).

Saying Good Night

Most children have fairly consistent routines when it comes to those final moments before saying good night, including turning down the sheets, climbing into bed, fluffing their pillow, organizing their stuffed animals, turning on night lights, and giving hugs and kisses to end the day. All these things can be counted, and adding a routine count to some of these items can make for a more predictable pattern of events related to saying good night. A light on a timer is also a very useful. Children can count to the highest number they know in anticipation of the light going out. Here are some sample bedtime dialogues:

· Okay, one blankie, two blankies. One bear, two bears, three bears. How many bears? One hug, and three kisses. One, two, three. Good night! Count to the highest number you can to see how long the light takes to go to sleep.

- Let's blow a good night kiss to the moon. I'm giving you two kisses, one on your right cheek and one on your left. Give me two good night kisses too! Night, night. *(saying it very softly to indicate it's time for the adult to leave the room)*

CHORES AND HELPING

Young children typically want to help. All evidence points to the importance of letting them help and getting them involved in household tasks early on during childhood—even though their helpfulness sometimes creates more work for the adults!

Tidy Up!

Count everything during this cleanup activity. For example, ask children to pick up a set number of objects and count with them as they do so. This helps motivate them toward an end goal (i.e., a clean and tidy place) but also reinforces one-to-one counting and expanding the amount of number words they know. Besides counting a set number of objects, children and adults can even count the number of steps they each took to pick up each of the objects or to complete the cleanup task. Another strategy might be to name the shapes of the objects that the child is tidying up. Young children often struggle with atypical representations of shapes (Aslan & Arnas, 2007; Clements, 1999). For example, asking the child to pick up the objects by their shapes or their likeness to a shape or size can draw the child's attention to different kinds of shapes and sizes. This can make the task more fun and varied than just focusing on counting.

Laundry

Sorting laundry into piles of more or less, into different colors, by whose laundry it is, or by item characteristics (i.e., anything with two arm holes or two legs) is another way of reinforcing the counting principles. Another idea is to ask children to help put a specific quantity of clothing into the laundry hamper and then count with them as they do so. A very common task is matching socks—one, then two. For toddlers, this can be a particularly useful task to assist them in understanding sets of objects with a cardinality of two. Moreover, it is also useful for learning subitizing, given that the quantity is small enough that they can practice picking out two items without counting. Besides matching socks, you could also match pajama tops and bottoms, as seen in Text Box 6.2.

Gardening

The garden is a place where lots of mathematics learning can occur. Even gardening in patio planters can be a powerful learning setting for young children. Plants can be measured for growth, water can be measured for watering, and plants and fruits produced can be counted. The number of seeds planted and those that blossom into plants, fruits, and vegetables could also be observed and counted, which is useful for instilling the one-to-one correspondence principle. Gardens can be arranged in rectangular beds and the idea of the rectangle can be discussed with the child. For example, in this "rectangle" or "square" (as opposed to "section"), we are planting tomatoes. Rows of plants can be counted and measured to determine which row is longer. Amounts of rain can be monitored and measured daily, and watering time durations can be tracked with a watch or a timer. We can also tally the number of days on a calendar to keep track of the plant growth.

GROOMING

Very early in life, children start demonstrating an interest in grooming themselves and even their toys! Perhaps an early example that many adults may have encountered is a child's interest in

---

 TEXT BOX 6.2.   MATCHING AND SORTING GAME

Sock matching game

Adult: Here is a pile of socks. Can you grab two socks? Let's count the socks!

Child: One, two.

Adult: Can you show me with your fingers how many you have?

Child: *(raises two fingers)*

Adult: Great job! You have two socks. They make a pair of socks! Let's see who can find another two first.

The missing pajama top

Adult: Let's put all pajama tops here in a pile and all pajama bottoms there in another pile. How many piles do we have? Or which pile of pajamas has more? Let's count.

Child: *(counting)* This one has more PJ tops.

Adult: Oh dear, we should have the same/equal number of pajama tops and bottoms. Let's count again.

Child: *(counting with adult)* One, two, three . . . Oops, one PJ top on the floor. Now we have same-same.

Adult: Yes, great job! Now we have four PJ tops and four bottoms. Now we have eight in total.

---

holding a toothbrush as the adult tries to brush the child's precious new and few teeth. Grooming activities are great opportunities to engage in counting and other mathematics.

Dressing

Dressing provides ample opportunities to introduce numbers and even shapes to young children. Counting out clothes with a child helps the child learn about numbers but can also assist with organization. Counting body parts (e.g., one arm in one sleeve) as the clothing is put on is also very helpful. Buttons, pockets, zippers, and so forth can all be counted as part of dressing. There are also more creative opportunities that allow you to explore shapes when dressing. For example, circles, triangles, squares, and rectangles can be found on clothing as prints on the fabric or even as pockets or embellishments. Having a child lay out his or her clothing the day or night before is also an opportunity to engage in counting or even in spatial reasoning if the clothes are laid out in a specific configuration or space.

Hand Washing

Perhaps one of the most important aspects of hygiene instruction includes learning how to wash one's hands. This is another aspect of grooming that could be used to incorporate some mathematical talk. Children typically rush through this routine, much like they do with toothbrushing. Counting the squirts of soap and then counting to 10 while a child washes reinforces both counting knowledge and thorough hand washing! At the end of the washing, you can even check whether all the fingers are happily cleaned by counting each one.

Hair Brushing

Besides dressing, another grooming routine children can engage in is hair brushing. Children can count the number of brush strokes. This is an opportunity to learn to count well into the double digits—if the child can sit still long enough! For little girls, you can make ponytails or braids and count them. For our little boys, we could perhaps count the number of spikes if they have a funky hairstyle!

Bathing

Many children love bath time. Although this is an important time for water play, all sorts of counting can happen in the tub and in preparation for the bath. For example, children can count to three when helping to pour the soap to make bubbles in the tub. They can count the cups of bath soap, bubbles, and number of toys. A wall clock in the bathroom can assist with watching for time elapsed while in the tub. A clock is not routinely found in bathrooms but can be very useful with young children for learning time and keeping track of time in the tub, as can be seen in Text Box 6.3.

Toothbrushing

Besides fun bathing time, toothbrushing is another activity that children are familiar with, especially at bedtime. Encouraging children to brush their teeth long enough is sometimes a big task. A small egg timer can really help and can also assist with supporting young children in developing a sense of elapsed time. Young children can also count the growing number of teeth in their mouth as they brush each one independently or with help. Having an order to the brushing technique could also allow for a "first this tooth, second that tooth, third the next tooth" approach to oral hygiene.

ORGANIZATION AND TIME

Organization and time management tasks can be learned, and early childhood is a great time to begin. Using counting as the basis, young children can start to build lifelong organization skills and strategies.

Lists

From a very young age, children are encouraged to engage in activities that help them learn organizational skills and how to track time. Children can help by making numbered lists and then keeping track of things completed on the list. Stickers and pictures can be used instead of words for young children. Of course, the "one second, two seconds, three seconds . . ." or the familiar "one Mississippi, two Mississippi, three Mississippi" strategies that many of us use can also be an aid to help young children to keep track of time as well as learn their counting. Adults and children can invent their own counting strategies for tracking time.

Waiting

Children also spend a considerable amount of time simply waiting (e.g., to leave, to eat, while the adult gets ready, while the sibling is being tended to). Waiting times can become times for mathematical puzzles and challenges or even for simple games such as counting cars or rotating some sort of object. ECEs have typically not been trained to take advantage of the transitional time between routine events to create cognitive learning moments (Early et al., 2005). Thus it would not be surprising to see that adults in homes also do not make the most of a child's waiting times. Even a commitment to make waiting times mathematical will inject a considerable amount of number talk into a young child's life.

|||||| TEXT BOX 6.3.   MORE BATH!

One of the evening routines at Dayna's home is to sit her 11-month-old daughter, Colleen, down in the bathtub with her toys. Evening bath time is a favorite for Colleen and, as such, it is often difficult to get her out of the tub. As the water begins to cool down, Dayna says, "Two more minutes," to give the little girl a heads-up on what to expect. Mom holds up two fingers and then turns a small timer on the sink counter to the number two. She shows the timer to Colleen. Colleen continues to play in the tub. When the time goes off, Dayna says, "That's it! Ready, one (with a short pause), two (with a short pause), and three (with a short pause). Time to get out of the tub!" Colleen, who has also been learning sign language, immediately puts her hands together to gesture "more" to indicate that she wants more time.

Like most parents, Dayna can't resist the innocent facial expression, so she gives in. She resets the timer for another 2 minutes and shows it along with her two fingers to Colleen. Colleen continues to play and is ready to get out of the tub the next time the timer goes off—particularly now because the water is really getting cool!

Telling Time

Children are capable of coming to school with some ability to tell time and with the ability to talk about time elapsed. Schools do a better job of teaching time by nature of their daily structure. At home, children should be encouraged to think about time through simple discussions about the positions of the "big hand" and the "little hand" on the clock and considering the changes as opportunities to count from the smaller number or to engage in simple additive or subtractive dialogue. Some sample starters for conversations about time could include the following:

- The little hand is at 6. When the little hand gets to 8, we will have to get out of the tub. What number is the big hand at?

- What is the next number the big hand will move to?

- Look! It's now 3 o'clock. It was 2 o'clock when we had our nap. Two, three … one hour has passed.

- It is now 4 o'clock. The last time we looked at the clock, it was 3 o'clock. How many hours have passed?

First This, Second That

We started this chapter with the simple yet powerful idea of changing the typical "first this, then that" wording to "first this, second that" wording to promote learning of the ordinality principle. This is a powerful shift that can be used to incorporate ordinal numbers into any routine task.

CHAPTER SUMMARY

Young children can do more, mathematically, than we think. Opportunities to develop a clear understanding of counting and some basic mathematics through routine activities have been shown to give young children considerable advantages at the start of schooling, and this advantage is sustained—some say throughout college. Schooling does not necessarily close the gap between those children that come to school mathematically ready and those who do not. Numbers and basic mathematics can be and should be infused in the everyday activities of a child. Such infusion requires intentionality on behalf of the adult, and this intentionality should be motivated by the lasting benefits that have been shown to emerge for those children who come to school mathematically ready. Interaction and sensitivity to developmentally appropriate learning are the keys to laying the foundation of early mathematics learning.

7

Mathematics Education During Formal Schooling

The start of first grade can be a time of great transition for a child and his or her adult caregivers. As a parent, teacher, or caregiver, take time to look around your child's school. Look at what's on the walls and in the hallways. What matters most to a school community is often displayed on the walls or even quickly upon entry into the school. Can you see mathematics on the walls, displayed and presented as proudly as students' work in other subjects? Mathematics is often not displayed as important learning pieces in public places. Why is this the case? What does this mean?

In this chapter, we briefly discuss some of important findings related to formal schooling—things that are helpful for parents, caregivers, and early childhood educators (ECEs) to know. Each of the topics discussed here could be chapters or entire books on their own—and indeed they are! Our intention here is to recognize their importance and to draw attention to the complexities associated with formal schooling that may be relevant for a child, parent, caregiver, ECE, or teacher. For example, we will talk about culturally responsive pedagogy and teaching to highlight the fact that a child's understanding of language is not the same as his or her understanding of mathematics or any other content area. An impairment in language abilities is not necessarily an impairment in mathematics abilities. Unfortunately, this has historically been an issue that is misdiagnosed for children who come to school with a first language that is different from the language of instruction.

We also discuss children's readiness for schooling and the important steps teachers and parents can take to provide support for children who come to school without a good understanding of counting and numbers. Our coverage of these important topics is brief, but we believe they are important to bring to our readers' attention as we conclude this book and as LittleCounters begin school.

NATIONAL COUNCIL OF TEACHERS OF MATHEMATICS

A central guiding body for mathematics education in the United States and even internationally is the National Council of Teachers of Mathematics (NTCM), whom we have mentioned many times throughout this book. This council, made up of mathematics teachers, educators, researchers, and policy makers, provides important international leadership on all issues related to mathematics education from prekindergarten to Grade 12.

The National Council of Teachers of Mathematics' (NCTM's) *Principles and Standards for School Mathematics* (2000) is a foundational document for many jurisdictions and countries, outlining mathematical curriculum, teaching, and assessment practices from prekindergarten to Grade 12. Although many educators have knowledge of the work and the contributions of NCTM, parents, caregivers, and even ECEs may be unaware of this important council and this document. This document is a good place to start (see http://www.nctm.org) for parents and caregivers of children in schools who would like to know more about curriculum progression, grade level outcomes, and expectations. Parents, caregivers, and ECEs can also look at the standards of their local governing agencies responsible for education, such as the ministry of education or district school board.

The NCTM document outlines six key principles for mathematics education.

1. *Equity:* Excellence in mathematics education requires equity—high expectations and strong support for all students.

2. *Curriculum:* A curriculum is more than a collection of activities; it must be coherent, focused on important mathematics, and well articulated across the grades.

3. *Teaching:* Effective mathematics teaching requires understanding what students know and need to learn and then challenging and supporting them to learn it well.

4. *Learning:* Students must learn mathematics with understanding, actively building new knowledge from experience and previous knowledge.

5. *Assessment:* Assessment should support the learning of important mathematics and furnish useful information to both teachers and students.

6. *Technology:* Technology is essential in teaching and learning mathematics; it influences the mathematics that is taught and enhances students' learning.

Principles and Standards for School Mathematics (2000) also defines the content areas in school mathematics as 1) numbers and operations, 2) algebra, 3) geometry, 4) data analysis, and 5) probability. According to the NCTM, these content areas vary in emphasis throughout the curriculum at different times. The goal of this document is to ensure that the materials taught in school are appropriate based on the students' developmental progression in their mathematical understanding. A significant emphasis is placed on numbers and operations during early schooling years between first and third grade. This is not surprising, given how important this content area is for future learning in other mathematical areas.

Besides the content areas, the document outlines the processes that are important for developing a good grasp of mathematics: problem solving (applying mathematics to solve a hypothetical or actual situation); reasoning and proof (making a meaningful mathematical case; for example, why Pythagoras's theory explains how the lengths of a right angle triangle are related); connections (linking ideas and concepts across mathematical strands; for example, using a ruler to measure instead of a nonstandard unit for consistency in measurements); communication (effectively conveying the mathematical solution or thinking orally or in writing); and representations (presenting mathematics in a variety of ways such as diagrams, equations, or graphs). The comprehensive list of content areas and processes that are recommended by the council reflects a widely held belief that mathematics education is more than just learning calculations. Being mathematically literate means being able to show both conceptual and procedural understanding and skills in different ways across different content areas.

Some, however, have started to question whether the expectations set out by the council for children are appropriately challenging. This question is a reasonable one—particularly given the performance of children from Western countries on international standardized tests. Western children are lagging behind children from countries such as Korea, Finland, and Singapore. Although jurisdictions may vary slightly on their standards and processes, there is an overall consensus on what should be included in the mathematics curriculum. Nevertheless, there are key differences between jurisdictions on *when* to introduce certain content and *how much* to include in mathematics curriculum. We will discuss these differences shortly, along with the implications of teachers and teaching methods for the mathematical achievement of students.

READINESS FOR SCHOOLING

If you are reading this book with a child already in school or perhaps approaching the start of schooling, you may be wondering,given the emphasis of the book on helping a child be as mathematically ready as possible before he or she starts school, whether or not you are already behind. You may be wondering what to do now that your child has started school.

Now that you have a better understanding of what is important, it is not too late to support your child's mathematical development. However, you should be aware that children who come to school less ready than they are capable of are at a disadvantage (Byrnes & Wasik, 2009; Duncan et al., 2007; Romano, Babchishin, Pagani, & Kohen, 2010). It takes some time to get these children "back on track." Literacy research provides some comforting evidence that children can get back on track by the third grade if appropriate reading intervention programs are put in place (e.g., De Jong & Leseman, 2001). The start of formal schooling is immediately an intervention of sorts, given that children can be doing much more mathematically before they start schooling if they are given the opportunity to do so.

It is important to note that developmental progression varies from child to child. The joint position statement by the National Association for the Education of Young Children (NAEYC) and NCTM (2002) states clearly that individual differences among children are common in terms of their developmental progression toward grasping mathematical concepts. Some children may pick up some concepts or topics more quickly and easily, whereas others may learn more slowly because of a variety of factors, even if a focus on counting, numbers, and other mathematics has been in place in the home or early childhood setting. The idea of a learning pathway or progression is meant not to suggest a strict time frame for learning but rather to give a realistic time range in which certain cognitive milestones should be seen in most developing children. That being said, significant deviations from milestones or an unusual inability to understand should be of some concern and is reason for parents and teachers to take a closer look at the child's learning behavior. For example, if a child is unable to count from 1 to 10 or is unable to identify numbers at the end of first grade, additional attention should be given to support this child's learning of numbers.

The NAEYC position paper on developmentally appropriate practices in early childhood programs for children from birth to age 8 states that early childhood education settings and elementary schools should have better ways of connecting, communicating, and collaborating (NAEYC, 2009, p. 3). Although there is another NAEYC and NCTM position paper on early mathematics learning (2002) and NCTM has also included early childhood education settings in its guidelines for mathematics education, instruction, and assessment (2000), we still do not know to what extent ECEs and elementary teachers actually collaborate and share experiences. Indeed, in many jurisdictions, including our own in Ontario, early childhood education records are not part of the official academic record that follows the child from the start of elementary schooling to the end of high school (i.e., age 17, Grade 12, or prior to postsecondary education). Thus elementary school teachers do not have a record of information on a child's early mathematics and other learning from his or her preschool years. It is often left up to parents to communicate with teachers or left up to teachers to find out for themselves how much has been learned when the child starts schooling.

For teachers, it is crucial to have some sort of baseline measure of a child's understanding of counting principles and learning capabilities at the start of schooling. Adults can use the following questions to understand where a child is in his or her mathematical learning. Here are some questions that need to be addressed:

· Can the child count up to 5 objects?

· Can the child count up to 10 objects?

· Does he or she repeat count?

· When asked "How many?" after the child counted, does he or she answer correctly?

· Can the child start counting from somewhere in the set, other than the obvious first object, and still count all the objects without repeat counting? Does he or she still know the cardinality of the set?

· Can the child identify numbers?

Checking for all these abilities should take no more than 5 minutes per child. This quick baseline check of counting abilities is an important piece of evidence to guide teachers in developing individual learning plans for children.

Other skills worth checking, if children can demonstrate ability to engage in rational counting, are addition and subtraction and some simple spatial reasoning:

· Can they do simple addition up to 10?

· Can they do simple subtraction up to 10?

A neat game is called "Making 10." In this game, children are provided with either a partially completed 10-frame, such as appears in Figure 7.1, or one that is empty. They are then asked, "If 10 is the answer, what would the other number in the box be?" Some additional suggestions would be to provide the 10-frame on a piece of paper with room for children to do additional work, such as making a drawing, to help them come up with the answers. Another suggestion would be to have counting blocks, such as unit cubes, available for those children who might need some objects to support their thinking. Children who have a rational understanding of counting will be more inclined to count or use some other strategy rather than just guessing. It is helpful for parents, ECEs, or teachers to note what methods each child used to complete the puzzle, if he or she used a method other than guessing.

By the start of formal schooling or by age 5, children should be able to engage in simple two-digit addition up to 10. An alternative to "Making 10" for subtraction would be to prove a partially populated table with 10 – _____ = _____ (a number from nine to zero). See Figure 7.1.

2	
1	
	6
7	
	9
3	
	5
	9
0	

Figure 7.1. "Making 10" with a 10-frame.

Shape recognition activities can range from patterning and puzzle games to matching tasks. This sort of quick check of a child's understanding of geometric objects can be done in any setting—home, early childhood education center, or school. Observation is essential to gauge the child's understanding.

The most important baseline measure of the skills described previously is the counting assessment. It is a crucial piece of knowledge that teachers need to have in order to plan appropriately for the child's learning. If the child does not show a clear understanding of the counting principles, building this understanding should be a top priority at the start of formal schooling. For parents, caregivers, ECEs, and elementary teachers, we strongly suggest continuing to build the counting principles outlined in Chapter 3 and including, where possible, mathematics language and learning opportunities. Although children's play has many inherent, naturally emerging features of mathematics (Seo & Ginsburg, 2004), adult interaction to support and advance the child's learning is critical and requires purposeful planning, integration, and engagement (Kotsopoulos & Lee, 2013).

NARROWING THE GAP

Children from disadvantaged backgrounds, including some children who are racial minorities, those living in poverty, or those who speak languages that are different from the language in which school is taught, have been shown to be particularly disadvantaged at the start of and throughout their formal schooling. There is compelling evidence that social and economic factors have an impact on mathematical learning, particularly for children from disadvantaged backgrounds. There is also clear evidence to argue for more resources to be devoted to early childhood education. For every dollar invested in early childhood, the return to the economic prosperity of a country and thus an individual is well into the double digits (Alexander & Ignjatovic, 2012; Heckman & Masterov, 2004). The return can be upward of triple for those children who are disadvantaged. Although the results are more modest for nondisadvantaged children than the return on investment for disadvantaged children, the returns of investing in early childhood are still impressive for any child (Alexander & Ignjatovic, 2012). All in all, investing in early childhood is a win-win situation.

These early disadvantages in learning seen in children from disadvantaged backgrounds grow exponentially throughout their formal education years. It becomes an increasingly complex challenge for educators, policy makers, parents, and society to bridge the gap later in life. To close the commonly known "gap" between those children that are disadvantaged and those that are not, all of us, especially our policy makers, must make early childhood education a funding priority.

The remarkable gains and outcomes in countries such as Finland, whose students consistently score well in international standardized testing, are important to consider. In particular, both children from disadvantaged backgrounds and those who are not disadvantaged show universal gains in mathematics achievement through the Finnish education system (Organisation for Economic Co-operation and Development, 2012). Finland's policies related to early childhood care and education from birth to age 6 are a key factor in their success in supporting children most at risk. All Finnish families have access to affordable and high-quality early child care and education; consequently, many Finnish children have the opportunity to experience enriched learning environments prior to the start of formal schooling. Other factors include the quality of the teaching in their schools, which we will discuss shortly.

As mentioned several times throughout the book, cultural differences between the ways in which children learn, play, and even understand mathematics are real. Much research exists on ways to support English language learners with mathematics. This growing group of children in Western cultures has been identified as perhaps the most at risk for falling behind in their education, followed by children from minority groups and then children from low socioeconomic status family backgrounds (Robinson, 2010). Among children who have English as their first language, African American children have been shown to be the most academically at risk compared with Caucasian, Asian, or Latino/Hispanic children (Delpit, 1998; Howard & Terry, 2011).

To help children from different cultural and linguistic backgrounds, culturally sensitive pedagogies/instructions have been introduced in schools, and this should be welcome news for parents and children. Culturally sensitive pedagogies emphasize the need for and the importance of teachers valuing the types of knowledge and the ways of knowing that children from different backgrounds bring to school. This is particularly important for parents who are still supporting their children at home, in that a child's background and family life will not be ignored in planning for that child's learning.

Teachers could still be more effective in adapting their teaching methods to support these children in their learning (Gay, 2000; Sleeter, 2011). For example, children who come to school without a good knowledge of the English language often have their lack of mastery of English misunderstood or even assessed inappropriately as learning difficulties (Robinson, 2010). Teachers' assessments of a student's understanding of mathematical content, rather than his or her understanding of the language of instruction, require a different approach—one that allows for nonverbal engagement with concepts. Even a simple Internet search about the child's country of origin can be very revealing to teachers and can tell them more about what prior knowledge might be expected. The implications for a student's future are profound if teachers fail to adequately engage in culturally sensitive pedagogies to support all children's learning and development.

GENDER AND MATHEMATICS

It might still come as a surprise to most of us to know that many adults and children as young as 6 years old still hold mathematics-related stereotypes such as "Math is for boys, and not for girls" in our North American culture (Lummis & Stevenson, 1990; Nosek et al., 2009). Some evidence has been found in terms of gender differences between males and females in spatial reasoning as early as age 4 (Casey, Dearing, Vasilyeva, Ganley, & Tine, 2011; Levine, Huttenlocher, Taylor, & Langrock, 1999; Levine, Ratliff, Huttenlocher, & Cannon, 2011). However, it is promising to note that these gender differences have also been shown to be highly malleable in that improvements can be made to spatial reasoning with increased opportunities in a child's environment (Newcombe & Frick, 2010; Uttal et al., 2013). Spatial reasoning aside, for the most part, there is little evidence showing gender differences in mathematical competence in young children. Gender differences are mostly myths. Yet, unfortunately, many people still think that males are more competent than females in mathematics (Dickhauser & Meyer, 2006; Lloyd, Walsh, & Yailagh, 2005; Manger & Eikeland, 1998; Stipek & Gralinski, 1991).

Such mathematics-related stereotypes have been shown to negatively affect girls' and women's mathematics performance, even if they do not explicitly express or support the stereotypes (e.g., Ambady, Shih, Kim, & Pittinsky, 2001). For example, Ambady and colleagues (2001) found that when gender was highlighted for children 5–7 years old (as well as 11–13 years old), girls' mathematical performance decreased, whereas boys' mathematical performance increased. In their study, gender was highlighted for the younger age group by asking them to color a picture of a girl holding a doll, whereas the older group was asked questions such as whether girls were better than boys in sports and whether they have more male or female friends. Their findings are further supported by other studies showing that girls in elementary school already rate themselves as weaker than boys in mathematics (Fredricks & Eccles, 2002) but not in reading or spelling (Herbert & Stipek, 2005; Heyman & Legare, 2004). Furthermore, first graders have reported that men like mathematics better than women do and that men are also better at it than women are (Steele, 2003). What is disconcerting is the fact that children already have such gender-stereotype beliefs as early as first grade!

Children's perceptions are shaped from a young age by the influences that surround them. Our research shows that parents, ECEs, and teachers of children between 3 and 5 years old rated girls as less competent than boys in mathematics but not in reading (Lee & Schell, forthcoming). However, there were no gender differences in these children's mathematics and reading abilities. Parents and educators are the primary role models for their children. We play an important role in nurturing our children's perception of their own abilities and motivation in their academic pursuit. For example, mothers who have gender stereotypes about mathematics have lower expectations of mathematical success for their daughters than for their sons (Jacobs & Eccles, 1992). Even fathers' gender stereotypes predict their children's grades in mathematics (Jacobs, 1991) and have an effect on the development of their children's gender stereotypes (O'Bryan, Fishbein, & Ritchey, 2004).

What can we, as parents, do to narrow the gender gap in mathematics? Understanding that most gender differences are constructed rather than real will undoubtedly help. Adults should avoid making comments such as "Math is not for girls," and "Boys are better in math than girls." Presenting positive feelings toward mathematics is also helpful. Finally, engage *both* sons and daughters in mathematical activities and games. Counting can easily be done with both dolls and dragons!

THE ROLE OF PARENTS

Parents and other adult caregivers are important partners in a child's education. Regrettably, teacher education programs often fail to adequately prepare teachers to engage parents in their child's learning—to work in partnership with parents. Teachers routinely keep parents in the loop on what's happening in the classroom in terms of mathematics curriculum at parent-teacher meetings. It goes without saying that communication with parents is important. However, communication with parents during parent-teacher meetings at report card time is not enough for parents to be partners in their child's education. Parents should be given opportunities to participate in supporting learning in the classroom at home. Keeping parents informed frequently throughout the school year is one aspect of parent engagement, but it is not the only way to keep parents engaged.

Through regular communication with teachers, parents can continue to be involved in their child's education even after children start schooling. We encourage parents to continue to talk about mathematics in the home environment, and they should also initiate discussions with children about mathematics happening at school or in the home. Of course, this can be a challenge for many adults.

Some parents have shared with us that, by about fifth grade, their child seems to surpass them in terms of mathematics understanding and in the types of mathematics activities he or she is doing in school. The key to this conundrum is for parents to remain open and positive and, most importantly, participate as colearners with their child. Indeed, many parents have told us that they are learning mathematics all over again in order for them to support their child's learning. This is can be both exciting and frightening at the same time.

Sometimes the mathematics children are learning in schools is taught in a completely different manner than it was when some adults were taught. We hear this often from parents! Seeing and knowing different ways of doing mathematics are important for learners at any age. Children are encouraged in school to be able to flexibly work with mathematical concepts, as it is important for learning. Of course, ultimately, children tend toward preferred strategies when solving mathematical problems, just like most of us do. Thus a parent showing a child how he or she understands the mathematical solution, especially in terms of how he or she is thinking about the problem, could prove very useful in supporting the child's emergent understanding. However, we caution parents not to talk about how the particular concept was taught differently back when the parent was a child or say the old approach is better than the current approach.

Likewise, teachers are also encouraged not to discount parents' ways of approaching and understanding mathematics. This is not to say that children, teachers, and adults should not be concerned with helping children develop more efficient or more elegant ways to think about mathematical solutions. It is the discounting of different ways of thinking that should be avoided. For example, a child should not be discouraged from using his or her fingers to come up with solutions during primary elementary education—or arguably ever! However, if finger counting is the only strategy the child ever uses, then there is a cause for concern and a need to support the child in developing more sophisticated ways of understanding.

A typical question that comes up for parents and teachers is related to mathematics homework. Various studies report conflicting results on the benefits of homework (Simplicio, 2005). What appears to be consistent across studies related to mathematics homework is that it is the nature of the homework, rather than the time spent on it, that matters (Kotsopoulos, Lee, & Heide, 2010). Specifically, if the homework assigned is "make work," it will be of questionable benefit to the child's learning and make it tough for the child to stay engaged. Such homework might include mathematical tasks that are well below the child's current level of understanding, or excessive in terms of what the child might need to become proficient, or motivated by the need to simply have some kind of homework for the child to do at home. In short, homework has to have a purpose that makes it worth doing for the child. In addition, parent involvement and engagement with his or her child during homework has been shown to be related to both increased mathematics achievement and increased completion of homework (Patall, Cooper, & Robinson, 2008; Pezdek, Berry, & Renno, 2002).

The amount of time parents expect children to spend on homework varies and can differ across cultures (Tam & Chan, 2009). For example, children from Asian cultures are known to spend more time on homework than children from Western cultures (Tam & Chan, 2009). Teachers often have a general "folktale" rule for homework—that is, 1 minute for each year of the age of the child. So if your child is 5 years old, then 5 minutes of homework is reasonable. However, studies have shown that time spent on homework does not conclusively lead to higher achievement levels (Dettmers, Trautwein, & Lüdtke, 2009). Homework can lead to learning outcomes for the child if the homework is relevant and appropriately challenging (not simply "make work") for the child to complete and if the parents are also engaged.

Parents might encounter teachers or schools that have adopted a "no homework" policy. Some schools build time into their daily schedule for completing schoolwork that is comparable to the types of tasks that would be expected during homework. Eventually, though, children will be assigned homework as they progress in their elementary education—most certainly by the time they get to secondary school.

What recommendations would we give to you as parents and educators about homework? We would recommend building in some structured learning time in the home—say 1 minute for each year of the age of the child—on a mathematical game, a piece of technology, quiet reading, and some creative writing during each weekday. Bedtime story reading, although valuable, is not considered structured learning time. Developing a habit of sitting down in the evening to a task aimed at some academic endeavor will help children develop the necessary skills such as attention and motivation to carry out homework when it is required as part of their academic experiences. A key role for parents in the home is to support their children in developing the kinds of study skills necessary to succeed in school.

TEACHERS AND TEACHER KNOWLEDGE

The state of school mathematics has received unprecedented attention over the past decade. Concern is growing in many countries about their mathematics performance compared with other countries. International standardized testing of children's academic performance has yielded important insights into to how children in the United States and Canada compare with children in countries such as Finland and South Korea, who consistently perform at the top of the world in mathematics.

In 2000, 2003, and 2006, Finland was the top achieving country in mathematics and the second highest achieving country behind Korea in 2009 (Organisation for Economic Co-operation and Development, 2012). In 2009, 17 countries had higher average scores than the United States on the PISA (The Programme for International Student Assessment; http://www.oecd.org/pisa): Korea, Finland, Switzerland, Japan, Canada, the Netherlands, New Zealand, Belgium, Australia, Germany, Estonia, Iceland, Denmark, Slovenia, Norway, France, and the Slovak Republic (National Center for Education Statistics, 2013; Organisation for Economic Co-operation and Development, 2012). The PISA is a standardized performance test of mathematics, science, and reading.

With such impressive records of students' scholastic performance, most of us might be wondering what the secret recipe to Finland's success might be. Finland's education system has a number of features that have been flagged as instrumental to their success in mathematics education:

1. High standards for teacher education (master's degree and subject specialization required)

2. Free access to early childhood education

3. Progressive teaching methods aimed at conceptual rather than procedural understanding

4. The autonomy of teachers to make decisions about curriculum and teaching, rather than a set curriculum mandated by the government

As we mentioned earlier, the outcomes for Finnish students in mathematics achievement are noteworthy and even more impressive when we consider the equally impressive learning outcomes for students who are economically and culturally disadvantaged. Thanks to this approach to education, Finnish citizens are making important gains in addressing the achievement gap in their country.

Teachers are prepared differently in different parts of the world. Specifically, all Finnish teachers are required to have a master's degree (Kansanen, 2003). They are also required to complete comprehensive research projects as part of their teacher education—a task that aims to promote a disposition among teachers to understand research and adopt an approach to teaching and learning that is evidence based (Kotsopoulos, Mueller, & Buzza, 2012). Admission to teacher education programs in Finland is highly competitive (Kansanen, 2003).

In many countries, teachers in elementary school or even at the high school level have little postsecondary mathematics training. Moreover, studies have reported that many teachers simply dislike teaching mathematics because of their own prior learning histories (Ball & Bass, 2001; Ball, Bass, Sleep, & Thames, 2005; Hill et al., 2008). Research from Finland suggests that the quality—in addition to the quantity—of teacher education significantly affects the quality of education that children receive (Early et al., 2007; Schmidt et al., 2007).

Many young people and even adults proclaim they are "bad" at mathematics. Very few people are actually unable to do mathematics—in fact, less than 6% (Butterworth, 1999a, 1999b). The reality is that after children start schooling, the quality of the teaching is one of the strongest influencing factors of student learning outcomes (Hiebert & Grouws, 2007). Given the less than stellar outcomes of many Western countries in international standardized testing, the pressing question we are asking is how best to educate teachers so that, in turn, they are better at educating children in mathematics.

In recent years, there has been an emphasis on preparing teachers with a fairly specific type of knowledge called "mathematics for teaching," which includes an understanding of pedagogy or teaching instruction, child development, and mathematics (Adler & Davis, 2006; Ball & Bass, 2001; Ball et al., 2005; Ball & Grevholm, 2008; Davis & Simmt, 2006; Hill et al., 2008; Kotsopoulos & Lavigne, 2008; Stylianides & Stylianides, 2009).

What does and should mathematics teaching in elementary school look like? What should you expect a young child to experience in his or her mathematical learning? The predominant view is that children should be given opportunities to develop deep understanding. As outlined by the NCTM, developing this deep understanding requires a particular approach to learning that involves discovery, asking questions, probing connections, and facilitation of both conceptual and procedural knowledge. This is known as a "constructivist" approach to learning. In this approach, children are active learners rather than passive receivers of knowledge (Clements & Battista, 1990; Glasersfeld, 1995; Twomey Fosnot & Dolk, 2001). One might see constructivist teachers using hands-on activities with geometric shapes to allow children to explore, for example, the Pythagorean theorem. Discussing and sharing mathematical thinking are also common activities in classrooms. It would seem that the days of worksheets and examples on the chalkboards are over.

On the other hand, alternative research suggests that guided teaching, rather than constructivist (also known as inquiry-based) teaching, is more effective for learning (Kirschner, Sweller, & Clark, 2006; National Center for Education Statistics, 2006). Guided instruction includes some form of teaching by the teacher, coupled with a demonstration or opportunities for children to engage in actual tasks. Guided instruction looks more like traditional teaching but also includes opportunities for children to actively engage with the content. After reviewing existing research, we believe that children need a careful balance of instruction that attends to both the content area and the students' individual learning needs.

Some memorization is useful in limited contexts—particularly when it comes to procedural knowledge like multiplication tables—once children fully grasp the mathematical concepts. Children need to be able to rapidly remember and apply some facts, and knowing these facts automatically is important. Memorization could channel more brain resources to focus on other aspects of the mathematical problem instead of tying up our minds trying to compute procedural facts that can easily be learned by heart. Learning some things in the ways in which our grandparents learned them should not necessarily be discouraged.

What is important is that teachers make informed decisions based on their understanding of their students, the curriculum, the content, and existing research to choose effective instructional methods that are developmentally appropriate for the children they teach. Training teachers from the onset to have a research disposition, similar to those teachers in Finland, is important. It is this level of autonomy that Finnish teachers have in deciding how to teach, along with a strong grasp of mathematical knowledge, that is proving to be crucial to a child's academic mathematics achievement.

CHAPTER AND BOOK SUMMARY

Very young children can learn much more than we think before they start school. In fact, children who have been exposed to mathematical ideas and mathematical language at home and who come to school with an understanding of basic counting do better in school than children who have not. The advantages of early mathematics exposure can still be seen even at the end of high school. The main message of these findings is simple: Counting and talking with your child about numbers matters for his or her future. Mathematical ideas and opportunities are present in every part of a child's life. Parents, caregivers, teachers, and ECEs engaged with young children in exploring mathematical ideas really make a difference.

Once children get to school, parental engagement is still very important. However, the quality of the teaching they receive at school is a critical factor in their learning. Teachers must be committed to mathematics education and be willing 1) to learn as much as they can about how to best support mathematical learning in their classroom and 2) to set aside their own prior experiences. Teachers who were not very good mathematics students themselves can still be exceptional mathematics teachers. It comes down to a willingness to change and to learn. In our training of future teachers, we have seen this change happen many times.

We have confidence that, with a clearer understanding of the role of counting and the role of mathematical language and opportunities prior to formal schooling, adults, caregivers, and ECEs charged with supporting young learners can facilitate life-changing opportunities for learning. We hope that the knowledge we have shared in this book will be helpful in introducing children to mathematics in their everyday activities before they start school. It is our firm belief that all children can be raised as LittleCounters.

Overview of LittleCounters

In this appendix, we provide an overview of the five LittleCounters workshop sessions. Our main pedagogical approaches are outlined in Chapter 3. Just as a reminder, we emphasize the approach of "Name It, Show It (and Say It), Touch It (and Say It), Move It (and Say It), Say It." We use our fingers to show a number whenever we say a number during our activities or when counting. We also emphasize again the importance of using developmentally appropriate sets of objects for counting. Typically, there are about 15 to 20 adults in each session, and each adult has one or more children with them.

Each of the five sessions typically follows this format:

1. Introduce, explain, and model the main concept.

2. Sing the "Welcome Song" (described later).

3. Engage in playtime, with at least one game, song, and poem that addresses the main ideas (described later).

4. Tell a story (see Appendix B).

5. Recite the farewell poem (described later).

The sessions typically last about 45 minutes each. Each family, upon their arrival, sits beside a "math tote," which contains play items for each parent–child pair to use during the session (Figure A.1).

Items in the math tote include (Figure A.2) counting links, toy vehicle counters, a collection of rubber fish, numbered bean bags, small numbered bowls, muffin tins painted with numbers,

Figure A.1. Typical room configuration for LittleCounters®.

Figure A.2.   Examples of toys and objects in a math tote.

a counting book, a counting puzzle, shape counters, a toy soccer game, a puppet, rubber ducks, and some sheer scarves. Items used are not restricted to what we have presented here. The items, songs, poems, games, and stories we use are meant to serve as suggestions for what adults can use with their young kids. Feel free to be more creative and find ways to have even more fun with your child!

We begin each session with the "Welcome Song" and use our fingers to model the numbers as we sing. The song helps us quickly learn the children's names, and the kids really enjoy hearing their names mentioned in a song!

Welcome Song (used by permission of Ell-Bern Publishing Co., ASCAP)
(Show numbers with your fingers.)
(Child's name) has one friend
One friend, one friend
(Child's name) has one friend
(Child's name) has two
(Another child's name) has two friends
Two friends, two friends
(Another child's name) has two friends
(Another child's name) has three

The song follows this pattern up to the number five. Then we return to the number one until every child's name has been included in the song. (Note that the reason we do not go beyond 5 or to 10 is because some of the children in the workshops are as young as 12 months old.)

At the beginning of each session, we introduce the concepts we are exploring, describe them in plain language, and then model the ideas with some of the toys in the math totes. We then engage in a variety of activities related to the topic, which include songs, poems, and games. In each of the following sections, we provide some illustrative examples. Many other activities can be initiated through a child's play that capture the same concepts. In addition, the activities we list under each workshop session can potentially be used on other days as well to illustrate concepts—they are not exclusive to the topics on that particular day, and they can be adapted to other topics. During some of the sessions, we also use a knitted puppet theater, which can be used with any of the poems and songs as well. We conclude each session by reading a counting book. A list of suggested books is listed in Appendix B. We then conclude with the "Farewell Poem."

Farewell Poem
(Show numbers and counting with your fingers.)
Five fingers saying good-bye friends
Five fingers saying see you again!
1, 2, 3, 4, 5!

WORKSHOP SESSION 1

Mathematical Concepts Introduced

1. One-to-one correspondence
   - Counting everything once and only once: no repeat counting
2. Magnitude
   - Comparing sets (e.g., Set A is smaller than Set B), using sets with clear distinctions or ratios of 1:2 to begin with

Suggested Activities

1. **Miniature soccer game**
   - Introduce the ideas of magnitude and comparison of sets.
   - Model one-to-one counting.
   - Position the pylons in sets of 1:2.
   - Ask the child, "Which one has more?"
   - After the child responds, count the objects.
   - Roll the ball.
   - Repeat.

2. **Go fish game (or "Go sea animals game")**
   - Use two bowls and the rubber fish.
   - Put one fish in one bowl and two fish in a second bowl.
   - Ask the child, "Which one has more?"
   - After the child has responded, count the fish.

(continued)

3. **"Ten Little Fingers" (song)**
(Show numbers and counting on hands; can be modified to only go up to five.)

One little
Two little
Three little fingers

Four little
Five little fingers

Six little
Seven little
Eight little fingers
Nine and 10 little fingers in a row!

4. **"One, Two, Three Fish" (poem)**
(Show numbers and counting on hands.)

One, two, three, four, five, once I caught a fish alive
Six, seven, eight, nine, ten, then I let it go again

Why did you let it go?
'Cause it bit my finger so
Which finger did it bite?
Little finger on the right

One, two, three, four, five, once I caught a fish alive
Six, seven, eight, nine, ten, then I let it go again

5. **"Here Is a Beehive" (poem)**
(Show numbers and counting on hands; clench fist and bring out fingers quickly one by one.)

Here is a beehive,
Where are the bees?
Hidden away where nobody sees.
Watch and you'll see them come out of their hives,
One, two, three, four, five, buzz, buzz, buzz.

6. **"Three Chirping Birds" (to the tune of "Three Blind Mice")**
(Show numbers and counting on hands.)

Three chirping birds, three chirping birds
Flying in the sky, Flying in the sky
They all flew up to the top of the tree,
And yelled down to mommy, "Hey look at me!"
Mommy said, "You flew so high I can see"
Three chirping birds

Three chirping birds, three chirping birds
Flying in the sky, Flying in the sky
They went to dig for worms one day
They got lost going the complete wrong way
They were late for bed and knew what mommy would say
Three chirping birds

Three chirping birds, three chirping birds
Flying in the sky, Flying in the sky
They love to count, it is so much fun
One, Two, Three birds lying in the sun
Birds like to have fun, so they also like to count
Three chirping birds

WORKSHOP SESSION 2

Mathematical Concepts Introduced

1. Stable order
   - "One, two, three, four, five, six, seven, eight, nine, and ten."
2. Abstraction
   - Knowing that everything and anything can be counted
3. Symbols
   - Identifying Roman numerals up to 10

Suggested Activities

1. **Let's line up the numbers (game)**
   - Use anything numbered.
   - Identify the numbers and put them in order.

2. **"This Old Man" (song)**
   (Show numbers and counting on hands; show gestures related to the song.)

   This old man, he played one
   He played knick-knack on my thumb
   With a knick-knack patty whack *(clap and pat lap)*
   Give a dog a bone
   This old man came rolling home. *(do a rolling motion)*

   This old man, he played two
   He played knick-knack on my shoe
   With a knick-knack patty whack
   Give a dog a bone
   This old man came rolling home.

   This old man, he played three
   He played knick-knack on my knee
   With a knick-knack patty whack
   Give a dog a bone
   This old man came rolling home.

   This old man, he played four
   He played knick-knack on my door
   With a knick-knack patty whack

Give a dog a bone
This old man came rolling home.

This old man, he played five
He played knick-knack on my hide
With a knick-knack patty whack
Give a dog a bone
This old man came rolling home.

This old man, he played six
He played knick-knack on my sticks
With a knick-knack patty whack
Give a dog a bone
This old man came rolling home.

This old man, he played seven
He played knick-knack up in heaven
With a knick-knack patty whack
Give a dog a bone
This old man came rolling home.

This old man, he played eight
He played knick-knack on my gate
With a knick-knack patty whack
Give a dog a bone
This old man came rolling home.

This old man, he played nine
He played knick-knack on my spine
With a knick-knack patty whack
Give a dog a bone
This old man came rolling home.

This old man, he played 10
He played knick-knack once again
With a knick-knack patty whack
Give a dog a bone
This old man came rolling home.
With a knick-knack patty whack
Give a dog a bone
This old man came rolling home.

3. **Magic numbers (game)**
    - Put number shapes or even bean bags with numbers on them in a bag.
    - As the child pulls them out, organize them from left to right from smallest to largest, focusing on the symbol but also the magnitude.

(continued)

4. **"Ladybug Rap" (used by permission of Music with Mar., Inc.)**
   (Show numbers and counting on hands.)

   See my hand? What's inside? *(make fist)*
   One little ladybug with a place to hide.

   There's something else. What should I do?
   Peek inside. Look, there are two!

   These little ladybugs are playing with me.
   Let's look again. Oops! There's three!

   Just when I'm thinking, "Can there be more?"
   I feel a little wiggle. Look, there are four!

   Let's wait and see if another will arrive.
   Hmm . . . yes! There's five!

5. **"Five Little Fish" (poem; used by permission of Hop 2 It Music)**
   (Show numbers and counting on hands; hold up your hand and move your fingers to the beat.)

   These are the fish swimming in the sea
   When we start out, let me see just one
   Whoops, say "hello" means another fish has come

   One little fish swimming in the sea
   Splishing and a-splashing, rockin' to the beat
   Here comes another fish, whoops, say "hello"
   Two little fish swimming in a row

   Two little fish swimming in the sea
   Splishing and a-splashing, rockin' to the beat
   Here comes another fish, whoops, say "hello"
   Three little fish swimming in a row

   Three little fish swimming in the sea
   Splishing and a-splashing, rockin' to the beat
   Here comes another fish, whoops, say "hello"
   Four little fish swimming in a row

   Four little fish swimming in the sea
   Splishing and a-splashing, rockin' to the beat
   Here comes another fish, whoops, say "hello"
   Five little fish swimming in a row

   Five little fish swimming in the sea
   Splishing and a-splashing, rockin' to the beat
   Five little fish swimming in a row

   Let's wave good-bye 'cause whoops, there they go *(wave)*
   Let's wave good-bye 'cause whoops, there they go *(wave)*

6. **Number puzzle play (game)**
   - Pull number pieces out and put them back into the puzzle.
   - Start with the smallest and go to the largest.
   - Use fingers to model the numbers.

7. **"1, 2, 3, 4, 5, Jump" (song; used by permission of Dream English)**

1, 2, 3, 4, 5, jump!
6, 7, 8, 9, 10, jump!
1, 2, 3, 4, 5, jump!
6, 7, 8, 9, 10
(Repeat.)

Here we go
1, 2, 3, step forward
1, 2, 3, step back
1, 2, 3, spin around

1, 2, 3, 4, 5, jump!
6, 7, 8, 9, 10, jump!
1, 2, 3, 4, 5, jump!
6, 7, 8, 9, 10

Here we go
1, 2, 3, 4, 5, 6, 7, 8, 9, 10

8. **Green and speckled frogs (puppet play)**
(Show numbers and counting on hands. Note that this is a counting forward poem. Feel free to change this poem into a forward counting one!)

Five green and speckled frogs sat on a speckled log
Eating some most delicious bugs—YUM, YUM!
One jumped into the pool, where it was nice and cool
Then there were four green and speckled frogs.

Four green and speckled frogs sat on a speckled log
Eating some most delicious bugs—YUM, YUM!
One jumped into the pool, where it was nice and cool
Then there were three green and speckled frogs.

Three green and speckled frogs sat on a speckled log
Eating some most delicious bugs—YUM, YUM!
One jumped into the pool, where it was nice and cool
Then there were two green and speckled frogs.

Two green and speckled frogs sat on a speckled log
Eating some most delicious bugs—YUM, YUM!
One jumped into the pool, where it was nice and cool
Then there was one green and speckled frog.

(continued)

One green and speckled frog sat on a speckled log
Eating some most delicious bugs—YUM, YUM!
One jumped into the pool, where it was nice and cool
Then there were no green and speckled frogs.

9. **Bunny show (puppet play)**
(Show numbers and counting on hands.)

One little bunny, not knowing what to do
Another hopped in and then there were two.
Bunny, Bunny, happy today.
Bunny, Bunny, hop and play.

Two little bunnies singing in a tree
One hopped over and then there were three.
Bunny, Bunny, happy today.
Bunny, Bunny, hop and play.

Three little bunnies were hoping for more
One hopped over and then there were four.
Bunny, Bunny, happy today.
Bunny, Bunny, hop and play.

Four little bunnies sitting in the sun.
Four little bunnies having lots of fun.

WORKSHOP SESSION 3

Mathematical Concepts Introduced

1. Cardinality
   - Knowing that the last number counted is the total of the set and being able to give *n* number of objects when asked (e.g., "Can you give me three?")

Suggested Activities

1. **Scarf toss (game)**
   - Toss the scarves back and forth with the children while counting.
   - After each toss, ask how many they have.
   - When they throw the scarves back, ask if they can throw one scarf, then two scarves, then three scarves.
   - While counting each scarf, show numbers on fingers.

2. **"Johnny Pounds with One Hammer" (song)**
   (Show numbers and counting on hands.)

   Johnny pounds with one hammer
   One hammer
   One hammer
   Johnny pounds with two

   Johnny pounds with two hammers
   Two hammers
   Two hammers
   Johnny pounds with three

   Johnny pounds with three hammers
   Three hammers
   Three hammers
   Johnny pounds with four

   (can go to 5 or 10)

3. **Making the wiggly worm (game)**
   - Using chain links, add one at a time and count.
   - Take one off at a time and then count how many are left.

(continued)

4. **"The Farmer Plants a Seed" (song)**
    (Show numbers and counting on hands.)

    The farmer plants ONE seed
    The farmer plants ONE seed
    Hi-ho the merry-o, the farmer plants ONE seed

    The farmer plants TWO seeds
    The farmer plants TWO seeds
    Hi-ho the merry-o, the farmer plants TWO seeds

    (Continue to any number up to 10.)

5. **"The Peanut Song" (song)**

    A peanut sat on a railroad track,
    His heart was all a flutter;
    Around the bend came number 10; *(turn and hold up 10 fingers)*
    Toot toot, peanut butter. *(pull down like you are pulling a horn)*

    An apple sat on a railroad track,
    Feeling at a loss;
    Around the bend came number 10; *(turn and hold up 10 fingers)*
    Toot toot, apple sauce. *(pull down like you are putting a horn)*

    A banana sat on a railroad track,
    He wasn't afraid a bit;
    Around the bend came number 10; *(turn and hold up 10 fingers)*
    Toot toot, banana split. *(pull down like you are putting a horn)*

    A strawberry sat on a railroad track,
    Reading that Sam I am;
    Around the bend came number 10; *(turn and hold up 10 fingers)*
    Toot toot, strawberry jam. *(pull down like you are putting a horn)*

    A grape sat on a railroad track,
    Its heart going flim and flam;
    Around the bend came number 10; *(turn and hold up 10 fingers)*
    Toot toot, grape jam. *(pull down like you are putting a horn)*

    A tomato sat on a railroad track,
    Singing a little ditty;
    Around the bend came number 10; *(turn and hold up 10 fingers)*
    Toot toot, spaghetti. *(pull down like you are putting a horn)*

6. **"Here Come the Frogs" (poem)**
    (Show numbers and counting on hands.)

    One little frog jumps onto the log
    Can everyone show me one finger?

    Oh, here comes one more frog
    Now two little frogs are sitting on the log
    Let's count them: one, two
    Show me two fingers. How many did we count? One, two.

Oh, here comes one more frog
Now three little frogs are sitting on the log
Let's count them: one, two, three
Show me three fingers.

7. **"Zoom, Zoom, Zoom" (poem)**
(Show numbers and counting on hands.)

Zoom, zoom, zoom, we're going to the moon
Zoom, zoom, zoom, we're going to the moon
If you want to take a trip, climb up on a rocket ship
Zoom, zoom, zoom, were going to the moon
1, 2, 3, 4, 5, BLAST OFF!!!

WORKSHOP SESSION 4

Mathematical Concepts Introduced

1. Order irrelevance
   - Realizing you can start anywhere in counting objects and end up with the same number of objects

2. Parity
   - Understanding the idea of equal, or the same

Suggested Activities

1. **Musical numbers (game)**
   - Spread number mats out around the floor (can use anything numbered).
   - Play any song.
   - The game is like musical chairs; children and parents walk around the number mats.
   - Pause the song every couple of seconds. The child jumps on any number mat, and the parent counts with the child to that number using fingers.

2. **Counting muffins (game)**
   - Use muffin tins and chain links—pull out exactly six.
   - Have children count and place the chain link in the numbered cup.
   - At the conclusion, have each child count all the chain links.
   - Stress to the child that the *same* number of chain links are in every cup.

3. **"Five Fat Peas" (poem)**
   (Show numbers and counting on hands; do the poem twice using each hand and empha-size the sameness of the number of fingers counted.)

   Five fat peas in a pea pod pressed *(hold infant's hand in a fist)*
   One grew, two grew, so did all the rest *(put thumb and fingers up one by one)*
   One, two, three, four, five! *(count with your fingers)*
   They grew and grew *(raise hand in the air very slowly)*
   And did not stop,
   Until one day
   The pod went POP! *(clap hands together)*

4. **Two puppies (puppet play)**
   (Show numbers and counting on hands; have puppets jumping and playing.)

   Two puppies playing Hide and Seek.
   Two puppies take a peek!

One puppy!
Two puppies!

Can you count the puppies?
One puppy!
Two puppies!
Show me two fingers!

Two puppies saying, "Goodbye!"
Two puppies saying, "See you next time!"
One puppy
Two puppies!
Goodbye!

5. **"Three Balls" (poem)**
   (Show numbers and counting on hands.)

   Here's a ball *(make ball with thumb and index finger)*
   And here's a ball *(make ball with other thumb and index finger)*
   A great big ball, I see overhead *(put arms up and touch fingers)*
   Shall we count them?
   Are you ready?
   One, two, three *(make all three balls in succession)*

WORKSHOP SESSION 5

Mathematical Concepts Introduced

1. Abstraction
   - Knowing that anything can be counted

2. Ordinal numbers
   - First, second, third, fourth, . . .

3. The number line
   - Recognizing that counting typically starts from left to right

Suggested Activities

1. **What comes first? (game)**
   - Put anything numbered into a bag and call this the "magic number bag."
   - Pull out the numbered objects one by one.
   - Organize them in order (e.g., "This is the number two. It is second, after the number one.").

2. **"One Potato, Two Potato" (song)**
   (Show numbers and counting on hands.)

   One potato, two potato,
   Three potato, four,
   Five potato, six potato,
   Seven potato, more!

   One potato, two potato,
   Three potato, four,
   One, two, three, four
   Five potato, six potato,
   Seven potato, more!

   One potato, two potato,
   Three potato, four,
   Five potato, six potato,
   Seven potato, more!

   One potato, two potato,
   Three potato, four,
   One, two, three, four
   Five potato, six potato,
   Seven potato, more!

   (Music interlude [Ask everyone to get one finger ready for one potato.])

   One potato, two potato,
   Three potato, four,
   Five potato, six potato,
   Seven potato, more!

   One potato, two potato,
   Three potato, four,
   One, two, three, four

Five potato, six potato,
Seven potato, more!

3. **Bean bag toss and catch (game)**
   - Ask which bean bag comes first.
   - Count the number of dots.
   - Toss the bean bag.
   - Ask which bean bag comes second.
   - Count the number of dots and toss the bean bag.
   - Repeat.

4. **"One Baby Fish" (poem)**
   (Show numbers and counting on hands.)

   One baby fish alone and new.
   Finds a friend, and then there are two.
   Two baby fishes swim out to the sea.
   They find another, and then there are three.
   Three baby fishes swim along the shore.
   They find another, and then there are four.
   Four baby fishes go for a dive.
   They find another, and then there are five.

5. **"Seashells" (poem)**
   (Show numbers and counting on hands.)

   One little seashell, all pearly new.
   Swish went the waves. *(open your other hand and pass it over the one finger)*
   Then there were two.

   Two little seashells, pretty as can be.
   Swish went the waves. *(open your other hand and pass it over the fingers)*
   Then there were three.

   Three little seashells, lying on the shore.
   Swish went the waves. *(open your other hand and pass it over the fingers)*
   Then there were four.

   Four little seashells, ready to dive.
   Swish went the waves. *(open your other hand and pass it over the fingers)*
   Then there were five.

Children's Counting Books

The following is a list of some counting books that are great for supporting LittleCounters. These books focus on counting forward, for the most part. Some do count to 10 and then count backward. We recommend avoiding counting backward until about age 5, or until you have observed that your child fully understands the counting principles outlined in Chapter 3, up to the number 10. Most of the books count up to 10 only, but some extend beyond. Only two books on our list specifically focus on ordinal numbers: *Ten Little Caterpillars* and *10 Little Rubber Ducks*.

Our own counting picture books are also included in this list. Our books have some unique features that have not been featured in other books. For example, on each page, we include the finger representations of the numbers, and each number is represented on a number line to show the relations among numbers.

A few of our favorite books are also included. We are both partial to Tony Bradman's *The Bad Babies Counting Book*, which is just plain fun, and the African-based counting book by Ifeoma Onyefulu, *Emeka's Gift*, which is culturally diverse. *Night Light* by Nicholas Blechman is particularly great for helping to establish one-to-one correspondence. The images in this book are in bright colors, and the pictures are simple to distinguish from one another when counting. Lynn Berry's *Duck Dunks* focuses on numbers up to five, and it is an appropriate book for those LittleCounters who are still learning numbers up to five. There are many more counting books. These are just some references from our collection and those available to us through our local library. Our library, for example, has all counting books labeled on a shelf with a "1, 2, 3," so it should be very easy for adults to find counting books for children.

OUR SUGGESTED LIST OF COUNTING BOOKS

Adams, M.M. (2010). *Counting cows*. Nashville, TN: Candy Cane Press.

Allbright, V. (1985). *Ten go hopping*. London: Faber & Faber.

Baker, K. (2004). *Quack and count*. Orlando, FL: Harcourt.

Barnett, M. (2013). *Count the monkeys*. New York, NY: Disney-Hyperion Books.

Bellefontaine, K., & Gürth, P-H. (2006). *Canada 1 2 3*. Toronto, Ontario: Kids Can Press.

Berry, L. (2008). *Duck dunks*. New York, NY: Henry Holt and Company.

Blechman, N. (2013). *Night light*. New York, NY: Scholastic.

Blumenthal, N. (1989). *Count-a-saurus*. Riverside, NJ: Simon & Schuster Children's Publishing.

Bradman, T. (1985). *The bad babies counting book*. New York, NY: Alfred A. Knopf.

Carle, E. (1969). *The very hungry caterpillar*. New York, NY: Philomel books.

Carle, E. (1982). *1, 2, 3 to the zoo*. New York, NY: PaperStar/Putnam & Grosset Group.

Carle, E. (2005). *10 little rubber ducks.* New York, NY: HarperCollins.

Carter, D.A. (2006). *How many bugs in a box?* New York, NY: Little Simon.

Charles, F. (2008). *The selfish crocodile counting book.* London: Bloomsbury.

Cole, N. (1994). *Blast off! A space counting book.* Watertown, MA: Charlesbridge.

Crews, D. (2011). *Ten black dots.* New York, NY: Greenwillow Books.

Dee, R. (1990). *Two ways to count to 10.* New York, NY: Henry Holt and Company.

Ehlert, L. (1992). *Fish eyes: A book you can count on.* Orlando, FL: Harcourt.

Evans, L. (1999). *Can you count 10 toes?* New York, NY: Houghton Mifflin.

Falwell, C. (1995). *Feast for 10.* New York, NY: Houghton Mifflin.

George, B., & George, J. (2012). *Number work.* New York, NY: Abrams Appleseed.

Grodin, E. (2006). *Everybody counts: A citizens' number book (America by the numbers).* Ann Arbor, MI: Sleeping Bear Press.

Hamm, J. (1994). *How many feet in the bed?* New York, NY: Aladdin Paperbacks.

Haskins, J. (1990). *Count your way through Canada.* Minneapolis, MN: Carolrhoda Books.

Honey, E. (2011). *Ten blue wrens: And what a lot of wattle!* Crows Nest, Australia: Allen & Unwin.

Hughes, S. (2001). *When we went to the park.* London: Walker Books.

Hutchins, P. (1986). *1 hunter.* New York, NY: Greenwillow Books.

Kitamura, S. (1999). *When sheep cannot sleep.* Singapore: Author.

Koller, J.F. (2003). *One monkey too many.* Orlando, FL: Harcourt.

Kotsopoulos, D., & Lee, J. (in press). *LittleCounters® around the world count.* J. Taylor Charland (Illus.). Waterloo, Ontario: Authors.

Lee, J., & Kotsopoulos, D. (2012). *LittleCounters® at the market.* A. Tumber (Illus.) Waterloo, Ontario: Authors.

Lindbergh, R. (2001). *The midnight farm.* New York, NY: Dial Books for Young Readers.

Litwin, E. (2012). *Pete the cat and his four groovy buttons.* New York, NY: HarperCollins Children's Books.

Long, S., & Grossman, V. (2013). *Ten little rabbits.* San Francisco, CA: Chronicle Books.

Lottridge, C. (2008). *One watermelon seed.* Brighton, MA: Fitzhenry & Whiteside.

MacCarthy, P. (1990). *Ocean parade.* New York, NY: Dial Books for Young Readers.

Martin, J.B. (2011). *Ten little caterpillars.* New York, NY: Beach Lane Books.

McGrath, B.B. (1994). *The M&M's counting book.* Watertown, MA: Charlesbridge.

McGrath, B.B., & McGrath, W. (2000). *The Cheerios counting book: 1, 2, 3.* Markham, Ontario: Scholastic Canada.

Merriam, E. (1999). *Ten rosy roses.* New York, NY: HarperCollins.

Murphy, S.J. (1997). *Every buddy counts.* New York, NY: HarperCollins.

Onyefulu, I. (1999). *Emeka's gift: An African counting book.* New York, NY: Penguin Group.

Pallotta, J. (1992). *The icky bug counting book.* Watertown, MA: Charlesbridge.

Pavey, P. (2009). *One dragon's dream.* Somerville, MA: Candlewick Press.

Pomerantz, C. (1984). *One duck, another duck.* New York, NY: Greenwillow Books.

Root, P. (2003). *One duck stuck: A mucky ducky counting book.* Somerville, MA: Candlewick Press.

Ryan, P. (1996). *One hundred is a family.* New York, NY: Disney-Hyperion Books.

Sayre, A.P., & Sayre, J. (2003). *One is a snail, ten is a crab: A counting by feet book.* Cambridge, MA: Candlewick Press.

Schwartz, B.A. (2007). *One to ten . . . and back again.* Nashville, TN: Candy Cane Press.

Sloat, T. (1995). *From one to one hundred.* London: Puffin.

Tripp, C. (2011). *Counting from 1 to 10: Les nombres de là 10.* Montreal, Quebec: Beaver Books.

Ward, J., & Marsh, T.J. (2000). *Somewhere in the ocean.* Flagstone, AZ: Rising Moon.

Ward, J., & Marsh, T.J. (2001). *Way out in the desert.* Flagstone, AZ: Rising Moon.

Children's Songs and Poems

The following is a suggested list of songs and poems that parents, caregivers, and early childhood educators can use to support their LittleCounters in their daily interactions. It is not a complete list, because we can only include songs and poems that are available in the public domain. Once again, as in Appendix B, we chose to include songs and poems related to counting forward. We have included the lyrics to make it easy for adults to use these songs and poems with their children. Remember to show the numbers with your fingers.

Baby Frogs

(Tune: "Mary Had a Little Lamb")

Tadpoles are little baby frogs, baby frogs, baby frogs.
Tadpoles are little baby frogs.
They can swim like fish.
Tadpoles grow four legs, four legs, four legs.
Tadpoles grow four legs.
They can hop, hop, hop.

Bee Hive

(Put your hand in a fist and say . . .)

This is my bee hive, but where are the bees?
Hidden inside where nobody sees.
Soon they'll come
Creeping out of their hive
One, two, three, four, five (pop fingers up while counting)
Bzzzzzz! (wiggle fingers around like bees escaping)

Big Dinosaurs

(Tune: "Ten Little Indians")

One big, two big, three big dinosaurs,
Four big, five big, six big dinosaurs,
Seven big, eight big, nine big dinosaurs,
10 big dinosaurs!
They all lived a long, long time ago.

They all lived a long, long time ago.
They all lived a long, long time ago.
Now there are no more.

Five Little Bears: Counting Up
One little bear
Wondering what to do
Along came another
Then there were two! Two little bears
Climbing up a tree
Along came another
Then there were three! Three little bears
Ate an apple core
Along came another
Then there were four! Four little honey bears
Found honey in a hive
Along came another
Then there were five!

Five Little Bees
One little bee blew and flew.
He met a friend, and that made two.
Two little bees, busy as could be—
Along came another and that made three.
Three little bees wanted one more,
Found one soon and that made four.
Four little bees going to the hive.
Spied their little brother, and that made five.
Five little bees working every hour—
Buzz away, bees, and find another flower.

Five Little Fishes
Five little fishes swimming in a pool
First one said, "The pool is cool."
Second one said, "The pool is deep."
Third one said, "I want to sleep."
Fourth one said, "Let's dive and dip."
Fifth one said, "I spy a ship."
Fisherman's boat comes
Line goes ker-splash
Away the five little fishes dash

Five Little Leaves
Five little leaves in the autumn breeze, tumbled and rumbled in the through the trees.
The first little leaf said, "I am red—I shall rest in a flower bed."
The second little leaf, the orange one, said, "Turn me over—I'm on my head."
The third little leaf said, "I am yellow—I'm a happy-go-lucky fellow."
The fourth little leaf said, "I am still green—I am part of the summer scene."
The fifth little leaf said, "I am gold—I'm a sign it's getting COLD!"

Five Little Snowmen
Five little snowmen sitting on the ground, (pat hands on floor)
The first one said, "Oh, my, aren't we round!" (make circle with arms)

The second one said, "There are snowflakes in the air." (wiggle fingers above head)
The third one said, "But we don't care." (shrug shoulders)
The fourth one said, "Let's run and run and run." (pat hands quickly on the floor)
The fifth one said, "I'm ready for some fun." (smile)
"Whew!" went the wind (blow) and out came the sun, (make circle with arms over head)
And the five little snowmen knew their fun was done. (pretend you are melting)

Good Night!
One fluffy quilt on my bed,
Two little pillows on my head,
Three teddy bears to hold tight,
Four kisses from my mom for a restful night,
Five hugs from my dad,
And off goes my light,
Good Night!

One Friendly Dinosaur
One friendly dinosaur wanted to play peek-a-boo.
She found another, and then there were two.
Two friendly dinosaurs looked behind a tree.
They found another, and then there were three.
Three friendly dinosaurs went to find some more.
They found another, and then there were four.
Four friendly dinosaurs in the water did dive.
They found another, and then there were five.
Five friendly dinosaurs played in the sun.
They all ran to hide; now there are none.

One Potato
One potato, two potato, three potato, four!
Well, I made a batch of hot potatoes
Dropped 'em on the floor!

One, Two, Buckle My Shoe
One, two, buckle my shoe
Three, four, knock at the door
Five, six, pick up sticks
Seven, eight, lay them straight
Nine, ten, a big fat hen

One, Two, Three, Four, Five
One, two, three, four, five
Once I caught a fish alive.
Why did you let him go?
Because he bit my finger so.
Which finger did he bite?
The little finger on the right. Ouch!

Sing a Song of Numbers
(Tune: "Sing a Song of Sixpence")

Sing a song of numbers,
Count them one by one.

Sing a song of numbers,
We've only just begun.
One-two-three-four-five-six,
Seven-eight-nine-ten.
When we finish counting them,
We'll start them once again.

Ten Little Fingers

Ten little fingers, ten little toes,
Two little ears and one little nose
Two little eyes that shine so bright
And one little mouth to kiss mother goodnight.
Ten little fingers, ten little toes,
Two little ears and one little nose
Two little eyes that shine so bright
And one little mouth to kiss mother goodnight.

Two Little Blue Birds

(Often sung as "Two Little Red Birds")

Two little blue birds (hold one finger from each hand, or two bird puppets, in front of you)
Sitting on a hill
One named Jack (wiggle one finger)
One named Jill (wiggle the other)
Fly away Jack (put hand behind back)
Fly away Jill (put the other hand behind back)
Come back Jack (bring one hand back to front with finger up)
Come back Jill (bring out other hand)

Two Little Hands

Two little hands go clap, clap, clap,
Two little feet go tap, tap, tap,
Two little eyes are open wide,
One little head goes side to side.

References

Acredolo, L. (1990). Behavioral approaches to spatial orientation in infancy. *Annals of the New York Academy of Sciences, 608,* 596–612.

Acredolo, L.P., Adams, A., & Goodwyn, S.W. (1984). The role of self-produced movement and visual tracking in infant spatial orientation. *Journal of Experimental Child Psychology, 38*(2), 312–327.

Acredolo, L.P., & Evans, D. (1980). Developmental changes in the effects of landmarks on infant spatial behavior. *Developmental Psychology, 16*(4), 312–318.

Adams, M.J. (1990). *Beginning to read: Thinking and learning about print.* Cambridge, MA: MIT Press.

Adler, J., & Davis, Z. (2006). Opening another black box: Researching mathematics for teaching in mathematics teacher education. *Journal for Research in Mathematics Education, 37*(4), 270–296.

Alexander, C., & Ignjatovic, D. (2012). Early childhood has education has widespread and long lasting benefits. *Special Report: TD Economics,* 1–9.

Alibali, M.W., & DiRusso, A.A. (1999). The function of gesture in learning to count: More than keeping track. *Cognitive Development, 14*(1), 37–56.

Ambady, N., Shih, M., Kim, A., & Pittinsky, T.L. (2001). Stereotype susceptibility in children: Effects of identity activation on quantitative performance. *Psychological Science, 12*(5), 385–390.

Andersson, U. (2007). The contribution of working memory to children's mathematical word problem solving. *Applied Cognitive Psychology, 21*(9), 1201–1216.

Andres, M., Di Luca, S., & Pesenti, M. (2008). Finger counting: The missing tool? *Behavioral and Brain Sciences, 31*(6), 642–643.

Andres, M., Olivier, E., & Badets, A. (2008). Actions, words and numbers: A motor contribution to semantic processing? *Current Directions in Psychological Science, 17*(5), 313–317.

Andres, M., Seron, X., & Olivier, E. (2007). Contribution of hand motor circuits to counting. *Journal of Cognitive Neuroscience, 19*(4), 563–576.

Antell, S., & Keating, D. (1983). Perception of numerical invariance in neonates. *Child Development, 54*(3), 695–701.

Aslan, D., & Arnas, Y.A. (2007). Three- to six-year-old children's recognition of geometric shapes. *International Journal of Early Years Education, 15*(1), 83–104.

Bai, D.L., & Bertenthal, B.I. (1992). Locomotor status and the development of spatial search skills. *Child Development, 63*(1), 215–226.

Baker, S., Gersten, R., Flojo, J., Katz, R., Chard, D., & Clarke, B. (2002). *Preventing mathematics difficulties in young children: Focus on effective screening of early number sense delays* (Technical Report No. 0305). Eugene, OR: Pacific Institutes for Research.

Ball, D., & Bass, H. (2001). Interweaving content and pedagogy in teaching and learning to teach: Knowing and using mathematics. In J. Boaler (Ed.), *Multiple perspectives on mathematics perspectives on teaching and learning* (pp. 83–104). Westport, CT: Ablex Publishing.

Ball, D., Bass, H., Sleep, L., & Thames, M. (2005). *A theory of mathematical knowledge for teaching.* Paper presented at the 15th International Commission on Mathematical Instruction (ICMI) Study: The Professional Education and Development of Teachers of Mathematics, Aguas de Lindóia, Brazil.

Ball, D., & Grevholm, B. (2008). The professional formation of mathematics teachers. In M. Menghini, F. Furinghetti, L. Giacardi, & A. Arzarello (Eds.), *The first century of the international commission on mathematical instruction (1908–2008): Reflecting and shaping the world of mathematics education—Proceedings of the symposium held in Rome, 5th–8th March 2008* (pp. 265–276). Rome, Italy: International Commission on Mathematics Instruction.

Barbarin, O.A., Early, D., Clifford, R., Bryant, D., Frome, P., Burchinal, M., . . . Pianta, R. (2008). Parental conceptions of school readiness: Relation to ethnicity, socioeconomic status, children's skills. *Early Education & Development, 19*(5), 671–701.

Barnes, M.A., Stubbs, A., Raghubar, K.P., Agostino, A., Taylor, H., Landry, S., . . . Smith-Chant, B. (2011). Mathematical skills in 3- and 5-year-olds with spina bifida and their typically developing peers: A longitudinal approach. *Journal of the International Neurological Society, 17*(3), 431–444.

Barnett, W.S., Carolan, M.E., Fitzgerald, J., & Squires, J.H. (2012). *The state of preschool 2012: State preschool yearbook.* New Brunswick, NJ: National Institute for Early Education Research.

Baroody, A.J., & Wilkins, J.L.M. (1999). The development of informal counting, number, and arithmetic skills and concepts. In J. Copley (Ed.), *Mathematics in the early years, birth to age five* (pp. 48–65). Reston, VA: National Council of Teachers of Mathematics.

Barrett, J.E., Clements, D.H., Klanderman, D., Pennisi, S.-J., & Polaki, M.V. (2006). Students' coordination of geometric reasoning and measuring strategies on a fixed perimeter task: Developing mathematical understanding of linear measurement. *Journal for Research in Mathematics Education, 37*(3), 187–221.

Berteletti, I., Lucangeli, D., Piazza, M., Dehaene, S., & Zorzi, M. (2010). Numerical estimation in preschoolers. *Developmental Psychology, 46*(2), 545–551.

Bisanz, J., Sherman, J.L., Rasmussen, C., & Ho, E. (2005). Development of arithmetic skills and knowledge in preschool children. In J.I.D. Campbell (Ed.), *Handbook of mathematical cognition* (pp. 143–162). New York, NY: Taylor & Francis.

Blevins-Knabe, B., Austin, A.B., Musun, L., Eddy, A., & Jones, R.M. (2000). Family home care providers and parents beliefs and practices concerning mathematics with young children. *Early Child Development and Care, 165*(1), 41–58.

Blevins-Knabe, B., & Musun-Miller, L. (1996). Number use at home by children and their parents and its relationship to early mathematical performance. *Early Development and Parenting, 5*(1), 35–45.

Booth, J.L., & Siegler, R.S. (2006). Developmental and individual differences in pure numerical estimation. *Developmental Psychology, 42*(1), 189–201.

Boulton-Lewis, G.M., Wilss, L.A., & Mutch, S.L. (1996). An analysis of young children's strategies and use of devices for length measurement. *Journal of Mathematical Behavior, 15*(3), 329–347.

Bourgeois, J.P. (1997). Synaptogenesis, heterochrony and epigenesis in the mammalian neocortex. *Acta Pædiatrica Supplement, 422*, 27–33.

Bowman, B.M., Donovan, S., Burns, M.S. (Eds.). (2000). *Eager to learn: Educating our preschoolers.* Washington, DC: National Academy of Sciences.

Brannon, E. (2002). The development of ordinal numerical knowledge in infancy. *Cognition, 83*(3), 223–240.

Brooker, L. (2010). Learning to play in a cultural context. In P. Broadhead, J. Howard, & E. Wood (Eds.), *Play and learning in the early years* (pp. 27–42). Thousand Oaks, CA: Sage Publications.

Burchinal, M., Howes, C., Pianta, R., Bryant, D., Early, D., Clifford, R., . . . & Barbarin, O. (2008). Predicting child outcomes at the end of kindergarten from the quality of pre-kindergarten teacher-child interactions and instruction. *Applied Developmental Science, 12*(3), 140–153.

Butterworth, B. (1999a). *The mathematical brain.* London: Macmillan.

Butterworth, B. (1999b). *What counts: How every brain is hardwired for math.* New York, NY: Free Press.

Butterworth, B. (2005). The development of arithmetical abilities. *Journal of Child Psychology and Psychiatry, 46*(1), 3–18.

Byrnes, J.P., & Wasik, B.A. (2009). Factors predictive of mathematics achievement in kindergarten, first and third grades: An opportunity–propensity analysis. *Contemporary Educational Psychology, 34*(2), 167–183.

Canadian Association for Young Children (CAYC). (2001). Position paper: Play for school age children. Retrieved from http://cayc.ca/pdf/playstmnt/pssachild.pdf

Cannon, J., & Ginsburg, H.P. (2008). "Doing the math": Maternal beliefs about early mathematics versus language learning. *Early Education & Development, 19*(2), 238–260.

Cannon, J., Levine, S.C., & Huttenlocher, J. (2007). *Sex difference in the early puzzle play and mental rotations skill.* Paper presented at a meeting of the Society for Research on Child Development, Boston, MA.

Carey, S. (2009). *The origin of concepts.* New York, NY: Oxford University Press.

Casey, B.M., Andrews, N., Schindler, H., Kersh, J.E., Samper, A., & Copley, J. (2008). The development of spatial skills through interventions involving block building activities. *Cognition & Instruction, 26*(3), 269–309.

Casey, B.M., Dearing, E., Vasilyeva, M., Ganley, C.M., & Tine, M. (2011). Spatial and numerical predictors of measurement performance: The moderating effects of community income and gender. *Journal of Educational Psychology, 103*(2), 296–311.

Casey, B., Erkut, S., Ceder, I., & Young, J.M. (2008). Use of a storytelling context to improve girls' and boys' geometry skills in kindergarten. *Journal of Applied Developmental Psychology, 29*(1), 29–48.

Charlesworth, R., & Leali, S. (2012). Using problem solving to assess young children's mathematics knowledge. *Early Childhood Education Journal, 39*(6), 373–382.

Clearfield, M.W. (2004). The role of crawling and walking experience in infant spatial memory. *Journal of Experimental Child Psychology, 89*(3), 214–241.

Clements, D.H. (1999). Geometric and spatial thinking in early childhood education. In D.H. Clements, J. Sarama, & A.-M. DiBiase (Eds.), *Engaging young children in mathematics: Standards for early childhood mathematics education* (pp. 267–298). Mahwah, NJ: Lawrence Erlbaum Associates.

Clements, D.H. (2004). Geometric and spatial thinking in early childhood education. In D.H. Clements, J. Sarama, & A.-M. DiBiase (Eds.), *Engaging young children in mathematics: Standards for early childhood mathematics education* (pp. 267–297). Mahwah, NJ: Lawrence Erlbaum Associates.

Clements, D.H., & Battista, M. (1990). Constructivism learning and teaching. *Arithmetic Teacher, 38*(1), 34–35.

Clements, D.H., & Sarama, J. (2007). Effects of a preschool mathematics curriculum: Summative research on the building blocks project. *Journal for Research in Mathematics Education, 38*(2), 136–163.

Clements, D.H., & Sarama, J. (2009). *Learning and teaching early math: The learning trajectories approach.* New York, NY: Routledge.

Clements, D.H., Swaminathan, S., Hannibal, M.A.Z., & Sarama, J. (1999). Young children's conception of shape. *Journal for Research in Mathematics Education, 30*(2), 192–212.

Colomé, Ã., & Noël, M.-P. (2012). One first? Acquisition of the cardinal and ordinal uses of numbers in preschoolers. *Journal of Experimental Child Psychology, 113*(2), 233–247.

Consumer Electronics Association. (2007). *Consumer perceptions of electronic toys.* Arlington, VA: Author. Retrieved from http://s3.amazonaws.com/zanran_storage/www.toyassociation.org/Content Pages/799252030.pdf

Cook, S.W., & Tanenhaus, M.K. (2009). Embodied communication: Speakers' gestures affect listeners' actions. *Cognition, 113*(1), 98–104.

Coople, C.E. (2004). Mathematics curriculum in the early childhood context. In D.H. Clements, J. Sarama & A.-M. DiBiase (Eds.), *Engaging young children in mathematics: Standards for early childhood mathematics education* (pp. 83–87). Mahwah, NJ: Lawrence Erlbaum Associates.

Cross, C.T., Woods, T.A., & Schweingruber, H. (Eds.). (2009). *Mathematics learning in early childhood: Paths toward excellence and equity.* Washington, DC: National Academies Press.

Cunningham, P.M., & Allington, R.L. (1994). *Classrooms that work.* New York, NY: Harper Collins College Publisher.

Curtis, R., Okamoto, Y., & Weckbacher, L.M. (2009). Preschoolers' use of count information to judge relative quantity. *Early Childhood Research Quarterly, 24*(3), 325–336.

Davis, B., & Simmt, E. (2006). Mathematics-for-teaching: An ongoing investigation of the mathematics that teachers (need to) know. *Educational Studies in Mathematics, 61*(3), 293–319.

Dehaene, S. (1992). Varieties of numerical abilities. *Cognition, 44*(1), 1–42.

Dehaene, S. (2011). *The number sense: How the mind creates mathematics* (Revised and expanded edition). New York, NY: Oxford University Press.

Dehaene, S., Bossini, S., & Giraux, P. (1993). The mental representation of parity and number magnitude. *Journal of Experimental Psychology, 21*(2), 314–326.

Dehaene, S., Molko, N., Cohen, L., & Wilson, A.J. (2004). Arithmetic and the brain. *Current Opinion in Neurobiology, 14*(2), 218–224.

Dehaene, S., Spelke, E., Stanescu, R., Pinel, P., & Tsivkin, S. (1999). Sources of mathematical thinking: Behavioral and brain-imaging evidence. *Science, 284*(5416), 970–974.

De Jong, P.R., & Leseman, P.P. (2001). Lasting effects of home literacy on reading achievement in school. *Journal of School Psychology, 39*(5), 389–414.

Delpit, L.D. (1998). Ebonics and culturally responsive instruction. In T. Perry & L.D. Delpit (Eds.), *The real Ebonics debate* (pp. 17–26). Milwaukee, WI: Rethinking Schools.

Dettmers, S., Trautwein, U., & Lüdtke, O. (2009). The relationship between homework time and achievement is not universal: Evidence from multilevel analyses in 40 countries. *School Effectiveness & School Improvement, 20*(4), 375–405.

Dickhäuser, D., & Meyer, W.U. (2006). Gender differences in young children's math ability attributions. *Psychology Science, 48*(1), 3–16.

Dietze, B., & Kashin, D. (2012). *Playing and learning in early childhood education.* Toronto, Ontario: Pearson Canada.

Doyle, R.A., Voyer, D., & Cherney, I.D. (2012). The relation between childhood spatial activities and spatial abilities in adulthood. *Journal of Applied Developmental Psychology, 33*(2), 112–120.

Duncan, G.J., Dowsett, C.J., Claessens, A., Magnuson, K., Huston, A.C., Klebanov, P., . . . Japel, C. (2007). School readiness and later achievement. *Developmental Psychology, 43*(6), 1428–1446.

Duncan, J., & Lockwood, M. (2008). *Learning through play: A work-based approach for the early years.* New York, NY: Continuum International.

Early, D., Barbarin, O., Burchinel, M., Howes, C., Pianta, R., Winton, P., . . . Aytch, L. (2005). *Pre-kindergarten in eleven states: NCEDL's multi-state study of pre-kindergarten and study of state-wide early education programs (SWEEP).* Chapel Hill, NC: University of North Carolina. Retrieved from http://www.fpg.unc.edu/sites/fpg.unc.edu/files/resources/reports-and-policy-briefs/NCEDL_PreK-in-Eleven-States_Working-Paper_2005.pdf

Early, D.M., Maxwell, K.L., Burchinal, M., Bender, R.H., Ebanks, C., Henry, G.T., . . . Zill, N. (2007). Teachers' education, classroom quality, and young children's academic skills: Results from seven studies of preschool programs. *Child Development, 78*(2), 558–580.

Emilson, A. (2007). Young children's influence in preschool. *International Journal of Early Childhood, 39*(1), 11–38.

Emilson, A., & Folkesson, A.-M. (2006). Children's participation and teacher control. *Early Child Development and Care, 176*(2–3), 219–238.

Evans, M.A., Fox, M., Cremaso, L., & McKinnon, L. (2004). Beginning reading: The views of parents and teachers of young children. *Journal of Educational Psychology, 96*(1), 130–141.

Fayol, M., Barrouillet, P., & Marinthe, C. (1998). Predicting arithmetical achievement from neuropsychological performance: A longitudinal study. *Cognition, 68*(2), B63–70.

Fayol, M., & Seron, X. (2005). About numerical representations. In J.I.D. Campbell (Ed.), *Handbook of mathematical cognition* (pp. 3–22). New York, NY: Psychology Press.

Feigenson, L., Carey, S., & Hauser, M. (2002). The representations underlying infants' choice of more: Object files versus analog magnitudes. *Psychological Science, 13*(2), 150–156.

Ferrara, K., Hirsh-Pasek, K., Newcombe, N.S., Golinkoff, R., & Lam, W.S. (2011). Block talk: Spatial language during block play. *Mind, Brain and Education, 5*(3), 143–151.

Fias, W., & Fischer, M.H. (2005). Spatial representations of numbers. In J.I.D. Campbell (Ed.), *Handbook of mathematical cognition* (pp. 43–54). New York, NY: Psychology Press.

Fischer, F.E., & Beckey, R.D. (1990). Beginning kindergartners' perception of number. *Perceptual and Motor Skills, 70*(2), 419–425.

Fisher, K., Hirsh-Pasek, K., Golinkoff, R., & Glick Gryfe, S. (2008). Conceptual split? Parents' and experts' perception of play in the 21st century. *Applied Developmental Psychology, 29*(4), 305–316.

Fredricks, J.A., & Eccles, J.S. (2002). Children's competence and value beliefs from childhood through adolescence: Growth trajectories in two male-sex-typed domains. *Developmental Psychology, 38*(4), 519–533.

Freeman, N.H., Antonucci, C., & Lewis, C. (2000). Representation of the cardinality principle: Early conception of error in a counterfactual test. *Cognition, 74*(1), 71–89.

Fuson, K. (1988). *Children's counting and concepts of number.* New York, NY: Springer-Verlag.

Fuson, K., & Willis, G.B. (1988). Subtracting by counting up: More evidence. *Journal for Research in Mathematics Education, 19*(5), 402–420.

Gallistel, C.R., & Gelman, R. (1990). The what and how of counting. *Cognition, 34*(2), 197–199.

Gallistel, C.R., & Gelman, R. (1992). Preverbal and verbal counting and computation. *Cognition, 44*(1–2), 43–74.

Gay, G. (2000). *Culturally responsive teaching.* New York, NY: Teachers College Press.

Geary, D.C. (2006). Development of mathematical understanding. In W. Damon (Ed.), *Handbook of child psychology: Cognition, perception, and language* (6th ed., Vol. 2, pp. 777–810). New York, NY: John Wiley & Sons.

Geary, D.C., & Hoard, M.K. (2005). Learning disabilities in arithmetic and mathematics: Theoretical and empirical perspectives. In J.I.D. Campbell (Ed.), *Handbook of mathematical cognition* (pp. 253–268). New York, NY: Taylor & Francis.

Geary, D.C., Hoard, M.K., Nugent, L., & Bailey, D.H. (2013). Adolescents' functional numeracy in predicted by their school entry number system knowledge. *PLoS ONE, 8*(1), e5461.

Gelman, R. (1993). A rational-constructivist account of early learning about numbers and objects. In D. Medin (Ed.), *Learning and motivation* (pp. 61–96). New York, NY: Academic Press.

Gelman, R., & Gallistel, C.R. (1986). *The child's understanding of number.* Boston, MA: President and Fellows of Harvard College.

Gelman, R., & Meck, E. (1983). Preschooler's counting: Principles before skill. *Cognition, 13,* 343–359.

Gershkoff-Stowe, L., & Smith, L.B. (2004). Shape and the first hundred nouns. *Child Development, 75*(4), 1098–1114.

Gilmore, C.K., McCarthy, S.E., & Spelke, E.S. (2010). Non-symbolic arithmetic abilities and mathematics achievement in the first year of formal schooling. *Cognition, 115*(3), 394–406.

Ginsburg, H.P. (2010). Early mathematics education and how to do it. In O.A. Barbarin & B.H. Wasik (Eds.), *Handbook of child development and early education* (pp. 403–428). New York, NY: Guilford Press.

Ginsburg, H.P., & Baroody, A.J. (2003). *Test of early mathematics ability* (3rd ed.). Austin, TX: Pro-Ed, Inc.

Ginsburg, H.P., Cannon, J., Eisenband, J., & Pappas, S. (2006). Mathematical thinking and learning. In K. McCartney & D. Phillips (Eds.), *The Blackwell handbook of early childhood development* (pp. 209–229). Malden, MA: Blackwell Publishing.

Ginsburg, H.P., Goldberg Kaplan, R., Cannon, J., Cordero, M.I., Eisenband, J.G., & Galanter, M. (2006). Helping early childhood educators to teach mathematics. In M. Zaslow & I. Martinez-Beck (Eds.), *Critical issues in early childhood professional development* (pp. 171–202). Baltimore, MD: Paul H. Brookes Publishing Co.

Ginsburg, H.P., Lee, J., & Boyd, J. (2008). Mathematics education for young children: What it is and how to promote it. *Social Policy Report, 22*(1), 1–23.

Glasersfeld, E.V. (1995). *Radical constructivism: A way of knowing and learning.* Washington, DC: Falmer Press.

Goldin, G.A., & Kaput, J. (1996). A joint perspective on the idea of representation in learning and doing mathematics. In L.P. Steffe, P. Nesher, P. Cobb, G.A. Goldin, & B. Greer (Eds.), *Theories of Mathematical Learning* (pp. 397–430). Hillsdale, NJ: Erlbaum.

Goldin-Meadow, S. (2005). Gesture in social interactions: A mechanism for cognitive change. In C. Tamis-Lemonda & B. Homer (Eds.), *The development of social cognition and communication* (pp. 259–283). Mahwah, NJ: Lawrence Erlbaum Associates.

Goldin-Meadow, S., Cook, S.W., & Mitchell, Z. (2009). Gesturing gives children new ideas about math. *Psychological Science, 20*(3), 267–272.

Gordon, P. (2004). Numerical cognition without words: Evidence from Amazonia. *Science, 306*(5695), 496–499.

Gracia-Bafalluy, M., & Noël, M.P. (2008). Does finger training increase young children's numerical performance? *Cortex, 44*(4), 368–375.

Graham, T.A. (1999). The role of gesture in children's learning to count. *Journal of Experimental Child Psychology, 74*(4), 333–335.

Greenough, W.T. (1997, November). We can't focus just on ages 0 to 3. *APA Monitor, 28*(11), 19.

Griffin, S., Case, R., & Siegler, R. (1994). Rightstart: Providing the central conceptual prerequisites for first formal learning of arithmetic to students at risk for school failure. In K. McGrilly (Ed.), *Classroom lessons: Integrating cognitive theory and classroom practice* (pp. 25–49). Cambridge, MA: MIT Press.

Gunderson, E.A., & Levine, S.C. (2011). Some types of parent number talk count more than others: Relations between parents' input and children's cardinal number knowledge. *Developmental Science, 14*(5), 1021–1032.

Guralnick, M.J. (2006). Family influences on early development: Integrating the science of normative development, risk and disability, and intervention. In K. McCartney & D. Phillips (Eds.), *The Blackwell handbook of early childhood development* (pp. 44–61). Malden, MA: Blackwell Publishing.

Gutiérrez, R., Bay-Williams, J., & Kanold, T.D. (2008). Beyond access and achievement: Equity issues for mathematics teachers and leaders. *NCTM News Bulletin, 45*(3), 5.

Halberda, J., Mazzocco, M.M.M., & Feigenson, L. (2008). Individual differences in non-verbal number acuity correlate with math achievement. *Nature, 455*(7213), 665–668.

Hannula, M.M., & Lehtinen, E. (2005). Spontaneous focusing on numerosity and mathematical skills in young children. *Learning and Instruction, 15*(3), 237–256.

Hart, B., & Risley, T.R. (1992). American parenting of language-learning children: Persisting differences in family-child interactions observed in natural home environments. *Developmental Psychology, 28*(6), 1096–1105.

Heckman, J.J. (2004). Invest in the very young. In R.E. Tremblay, R.G. Barr, & R.D. Peters (Eds.), *Encyclopedia on early childhood development* (pp. 1–2). Montreal, Quebec: Centre of Excellence for Early Childhood Development.

Heckman, J., & Masterov, D. (2004). *The productivity argument for investing in young children* (Working Paper No. 5). Washington, DC: Committee for Economic Development.

Herbert, J., & Stipek, D. (2005). The emergence of gender difference in children's perceptions of their academic competence. *Applied Developmental Psychology, 26*(3), 276–295.

Hespos, S.J., & Rochat, P. (1997). Dynamic mental representation in infancy. *Cognition, 64*(2), 153–188.

Heyman, C.D., & Legare, C.H. (2004). Children's belief about gender differences in the academic and social domains. *Sex Roles, 50*(3–4), 227–259.

Hiebert, J. (1981). Cognitive development and learning linear measurement. *Journal for Research in Mathematics Education, 12*(3), 197–211.

Hiebert, J., & Grouws, D.A. (2007). The effects of classroom mathematics teaching on students' learning. In F.K. Lester (Ed.), *Second handbook of research on mathematics teaching and learning* (pp. 371–404). Charlotte, NC: Information Age Publishing.

Hill, H.C., Blunk, M.L., Charalambous, C.Y., Lewis, J.M., Phelps, G.C., Sleep, L., & Loewenberg Ball, D. (2008). Mathematical knowledge for teaching and the mathematical quality of instruction: An exploratory study. *Cognition & Instruction, 26*(4), 430–511.

Hirsh-Pasek, K., & Michnick Golinkoff, R. (1998). The intermodal preferential looking paradigm: A window onto emerging language comprehension. In D. McDaniel, C. McKee, & H. Smith Cairns (Eds.), *Methods for assessing children's syntax* (pp. 105–124). Cambridge, MA: MIT Press.

Hirsh-Pasek, K., Michnick Golinkoff, R., Berk, L.E., & Singer, D.G. (2009). *A mandate for playful learning in preschool.* New York, NY: Oxford University Press.

Holloway, I.D., & Ansari, D. (2008). Mapping numerical magnitudes onto symbols: The numerical distance effect and individual differences in children's mathematics achievement. *Journal of Experimental Psychology, 103*(1), 17–29.

Howard, J. (2010). Making the most of play in early years: The importance of children's perspectives. In P. Broadhead, J. Howard, & E. Wood (Eds.), *Play and learning in the early years* (pp. 145–160). Thousand Oaks, CA: Sage Publications.

Howard, T., & Terry, C.L. (2011). Culturally responsive pedagogy for African American students: Promising programs and practices for enhanced academic performance. *Teaching Education, 22*(4), 345–362.

Huang, Y.T., Spelke, E., & Snedeker, J. (2010). When is four far more than three? Children's generalization of newly acquired number words. *Psychological Science, 21*(4), 600–606.

Hunting, R.P. (2003). Part-whole number knowledge in preschool children. *Journal of Mathematical Behavior, 22*(3), 217–235.

Huntley-Fenner, G., & Cannon, E. (2000). Preschoolers' magnitude comparisons are mediated by a preverbal analog mechanism. *Psychological Science, 11*(2), 147–152.

Huttenlocher, J., Jordan, N.C., & Levine, S.C. (1994). A mental model for early arithmetic. *Journal of Experimental Psychology, 123*(3), 284–296.

Huttenlocher, P.R. (1984). Synapse elimination and plasticity in developing human cerebral cortex. *American Journal of Mental Deficiency, 88*(5), 488–496.

Inhelder, B., Sinclair, H., & Bovet, M. (1974). *Learning and the development of cognition.* Cambridge, MA: Harvard University Press.

Izard, V., Dehaene-Lambertz, G., & Dehaene, S. (2008). Distinct cerebral pathways for object identity and number in human infants. *PLoS Biology, 6*(2), 275–285.

Jacobs, J.E. (1991). Influence of gender stereotypes on parent and child mathematics attitude. *Journal of Educational Psychology, 83*(4), 518–527.

Jacobs, J.E., & Eccles, J.S. (1992). The impact of mothers' gender-role stereotypical beliefs on mothers' and children's ability and perceptions. *Journal of Personality and Social Psychology, 63*(6), 932–944.

Jeong, Y., & Levine, S.C. (2005). *How do young children represent numerosity?* Poster session presented at the Biennial Meeting of the Society for Research in Child Development, Atlanta, GA.

Johansson, E. (2004). Learning encounters in preschool—Interaction between atmosphere, view of children and of learning. *International Journal of Early Childhood, 1*(36), 9–26.

Johnson, J.E., Christie, J.F., & Yawkey, T.D. (1987). *Play and early childhood development.* Glenview, IL: Scott Foresman.

Jordan, N.C., Huttenlocher, J., & Levine, S.C. (1992). Differential calculation abilities in young children from middle- and low-income families. *Developmental Psychology, 28*(4), 644–653.

Kahneman, D., Treisman, A., & Gibbs, B.J. (1992). The reviewing of object files: Object-specific integration of information. *Cognitive Psychology, 24*(2), 174–219.

Kamii, C. (1997). Measurement of length: The need for a better approach to teaching. *School Science and Mathematics, 97*(3), 116–121.

Kamii, C. (2000). *Young children reinvent arithmetic: Implications of Piaget's theory* (2nd ed.). New York, NY: Teachers College Press.

Kansanen, P. (2003). Teacher education in Finland: Current models and new developments. In B. Moon, L. Vlasceanu, & L.C. Barrows (Eds.), *Studies on higher education: Institutional approaches to teacher education within higher education in Europe: Current models and new developments* (pp. 85–90).

Kirschner, P.A., Sweller, J., & Clark, R.E. (2006). Why minimal guidance during instruction does not work: An analysis of the failure of constructivist, discovery, problem-based, experiential, and inquiry-based teaching. *Educational Psychologist, 41*(2), 75–86.

Klein, A., & Starkey, P. (2004). Fostering preschool children's mathematical knowledge: Findings from the Berkeley math readiness project. In D.H. Clements, J. Sarama, & A.-M. DiBiase (Eds.), *Engaging young children in mathematics: Standards for early childhood mathematics education* (pp. 343–360). Mahwah, NJ: Lawrence Erlbaum Associates.

Klibanoff, R.S., Levine, S.C., Huttenlocher, J., Vasilyeva, M., & Hedges, L.V. (2006). Preschool children's mathematical knowledge: The effect of teacher "math talk." *Developmental Psychology, 42*(1), 59–69.

Kotsopoulos, D., & Lavigne, S. (2008). Examining "mathematics for teaching" through an analysis of teachers' perceptions of student "learning paths." *International Electronic Journal of Mathematics Education, 3*(1), 1–23.

Kotsopoulos, D., & Lee, J. (2012). LittleCounters®. Trademark 85392260 in the United States Trademarks and Patents Office, an agency of the U.S. Department of Commerce.

Kotsopoulos, D., & Lee, J. (2013). What are the development enhancing features of mathematical play? *An Leanbh Óg: The OMEP Ireland Journal of Early Childhood Studies, 7,* 47–68.

Kotsopoulos, D., & Lee, J. (forthcoming). Shape discrimination in two-year-olds.

Kotsopoulos, D., & Lee, J. (in press). *LittleCounters® around the world count.* J. Taylor Charland (Illus.). Waterloo, Ontario: Authors.

Kotsopoulos, D., Lee, J., & Heide, D. (2010). Mathematical tasks used in class and related homework problems: A comparative analysis of levels of cognitive demand. In P. Brosnan, D.B. Erchick, & L. Flevares (Eds.), *Proceedings of the 32nd annual meeting of the North American Chapter of the International Group for the Psychology of Mathematics Education* (vol. VI, pp.768–775). Columbus, OH: The Ohio State University.

Kotsopoulos, D., Mueller, J., & Buzza, D. (2012). Pre-service teacher research: Early acculturation into a research disposition. *Journal of Education for Teaching, 38*(1), 21–36.

Krasa, N., & Shunkwiler, S. (2009). *Number sense and number nonsense: Understanding the challenges of learning math.* Baltimore, MD: Paul H. Brookes Publishing Co.

La Paro, K.M., & Pianta, R.C. (2000). Predicting children's competence in the early school years: A meta-analytic review. *Review of Educational Research, 70*(4), 443–484.

Lavin, T.A., Hall, D.G., & Waxman, S. (2006). East and West: A role for culture in the acquisition of nouns and verbs. In K. Hirsh-Pasek & R.M. Golinkoff (Eds.), *Action meets word: How children learn verbs* (pp. 525–543). New York, NY: Oxford University Press.

Le Corre, M., Van de Walle, G., Brannon, E.M., & Carey, S. (2006). Re-visiting the competence/performance debate in the acquisition of the counting principles. *Cognitive Psychology, 52*(2), 130–169.

Lee, J. (2011). Size matters: Early vocabulary as a predictor of language and literacy competence. *Applied Psycholinguistics, 32*(1), 69–92.

Lee, J., & Kotsopoulos, D. (2012). *LittleCounters® at the market.* A. Tumber (Illus.). Waterloo, Ontario: Authors.

Lee, J., Kotsopoulos, Makosz, S., & Tumber, A. (forthcoming). Children's use of gesture and mathematics learning. *Cognitive Science,* revised and resubmitted.

Lee, J., Kotsopoulos, D., Makosz, S., Tumber, A., & Zambrzycka, J. (2013). Does playing with technology help toddlers learn their 1, 2, 3? In M. Martinez & S. Castro (Eds.), *Proceedings of the 35th annual meeting of the North American Chapter of the International Group for the Psychology of Mathematics Education* (pp.1185–1188). Chicago, IL: University of Illinois at Chicago.

Lee, J., Kotsopoulos, D., & Tumber, A. (2010). What is in adult mathematical talk? In P. Brosnan, D.B. Erchick, & L. Flevares (Eds.), *Proceedings of the 32nd annual meeting of the North American Chapter of the International Group for the Psychology of Mathematics Education* (vol. VI, 547–554). Columbus, OH: The Ohio State University.

Lee, J., Kotsopoulos, D., & Tumber, A. (forthcoming). How mathematical is parent-toddler play?

Lee, J., Kotsopoulos, D., Tumber, A., & Dittmer, L. (2009). *Amount of mathematical talk and the acquisition of number sense in toddlers.* Paper presented at the Sixth Biennial Conference of the Society for the Study of Human Development, Ann Arbor, MI.

Lee, J., Kotsopoulos, D., Tumber, A., & Makosz, S. (in press). Gesturing about number sense. *Journal of Early Childhood Research.*

Lee, J., Kotsopoulos, D., Tumber, A., & Makosz, S. (forthcoming). I know my 1, 2, 3! Does number-word comprehension precede verbal production?

Lee, J., Kotsopoulos, D., Tumber, A., McGregor, S., Stordy, C.-A., & Schell, A. (2010). *Can we increase adult mathematical talk? An evaluation of LittleCounters.* Paper presented at Development 2010: A Canadian Conference on Developmental Psychology, Carleton University, Ottawa, Ontario.

Lee, J., Kotsopoulos, D., & Zambrzycka, J. (2012). Does block play support children's numeracy development? In L.R. Van Zoest, J.-J. Lo, & J.K. Kraty (Eds.), *Proceedings of the 34th annual meeting of the North American Chapter of the International Group for the Psychology of Mathematics Education* (pp. 1028–1031). Kalamazoo, MI: Western Michigan University.

Lee, J., Kotsopoulos, D., & Zambrzycka, J. (2013). *Block play: Parental input predicts preschoolers' numeracy competence?* Paper presented at the Society for the Research of Child Development Biennial Meeting, Seattle, WA.

Lee, J., & Schell, A. (forthcoming). Gender differences in emergent mathematics: Perception vs. reality. *Sex Roles,* revised and resubmitted.

Lee, J., Zambrzycka, J.,& Kotsopoulos, D. (forthcoming). Block play: A predictor of preschoolers' numeracy competence.

LeFevre, J.-A., Skwarchuk, S.-L., Smith-Chant, B.L., Fast, L., Kamawar, D., & Bisanz, J. (2009). Home numeracy experiences and children's math performance in the early school years. *Canadian Journal of Behavioural Science, 41*(2), 55–66.

LeFevre, J.-A., Smith-Chant, B.L., Fast, L., Skwarchuk, S.-L., Sargla, E., Arnup, J.S., ... Kamawar, D. (2006). What counts as knowing? The development of conceptual and procedural knowledge of counting from kindergarten through grade 2. *Journal of Experimental Child Psychology, 93*(4), 285–303.

Levine, S.C., Huttenlocher, J., Taylor, A., & Langrock, A. (1999). Early sex differences in spatial skill. *Developmental Psychology, 35*(4), 940–949.

Levine, S.C., Jordan, N.C., & Huttenlocher, J. (1992). Development of calculation abilities in young children. *Journal of Experimental Child Psychology, 53*(1), 72–103.

Levine, S.C., Ratliff, K.R., Huttenlocher, J., & Cannon, J. (2011). Early puzzle play: A predictor of preschoolers' spatial transformation skill. *Developmental Psychology, 48*(2), 530–542.

Lipton, J., & Spelke, E. (2003). Origins of number sense: Large number discrimination in human infants. *Psychological Science, 14*(5), 396–401.

Lipton, J., & Spelke, E. (2004). Discrimination of large and small numerosities by human infants. *Infancy, 5*(3), 271–290.

Lloyd, J.E., Walsh, J., & Yailagh, M.S. (2005). Sex differences in performance attributions, self-efficacy, and achievement in mathematics: If I'm so smart, why don't I know it? *Canadian Journal of Education, 28*(3), 384–408.

Lummis, M., & Stevenson, H.W. (1990). Gender differences in beliefs and achievements. *Developmental Psychology, 26*(2), 254–263.

Manger, T., & Eikeland, O. (1998). The effect of mathematics self-concept on girls' and boys' mathematical achievement. *School Psychology International, 19*(1), 5–18.

Matejko, A.A., Price, G.R., Mazzocco, M.M.M., & Ansari, D. (2013). Individual differences in left parietal white matter predict math scores on the Preliminary Scholastic Aptitude Test. *NeuroImage, 66,* 604–610.

Matsuda, F., & Matsuda, M. (1983). A longitudinal study of learning process of duration estimation in young children. *Japanese Psychological Research, 25*(3), 119–129.

Matsuda, F., & Matsuda, M. (1987). A developmental study of the role of learning processes in duration estimation. *Japanese Psychological Research, 29*(1), 27–36.

Mazzocco, M., Feigenson, L., & Halberda, J. (2011). Preschoolers' precision on the approximate number system predicts later school mathematics performance. *PLoS ONE, 6*(9), 1–8. doi:10.1371/journal.pone.0023749

McCrink, R., & Wynn, K. (2004). Large-number addition and subtraction by 9-month-old infants. *Psychological Science, 15*(11), 776–781.

Meck, W.H., & Church, R.M. (1983). A mode control model of counting and timing processes. *Journal of Experimental Psychology: Animal Behaviour Processes, 9*(3), 320–334.

Miller, K.F., Kelly, M., & Zhou, X. (2005). Learning mathematics in China and the United States: Cross-cultural insights into the nature and course of preschool mathematical development. In J.I.D. Campbell (Ed.), *Handbook of mathematical cognition* (pp. 163–178). New York, NY: Taylor & Francis.

Miller, K., Major, S.M., Shu, H., & Zhang, H. (2000). Ordinal knowledge: Number names and number concepts in Chinese and English. *Canadian Journal of Experimental Psychology, 54*(2), 129–140.

Mix, K.S., Huttenlocher, J., & Levine, S.C. (2002). Multiple cues for quantification in infancy: Is number one of them? *Psychological Bulletin, 128*(2), 278–294.

Mix, K.S., Levine, S.C., & Huttenlocher, J. (1999). Early fraction calculation ability. *Developmental Psychology, 35*(5), 164–174.

Mix, K.S., Sandhofer, C.M., & Baroody, A.J. (2005). Number words and number concepts: The interplay of verbal and nonverbal processes in early quantitative development. In R. Kail (Ed.), *Advances in child development and behavior* (Vol. 33, pp. 305–345). New York, NY: Academic Press.

Moomaw, S. (2011). *Teaching mathematics in early childhood.* Baltimore, MD: Paul H. Brookes Publishing Co.

Moomaw, S., & Heronymus, B. (1995). *More than counting.* St. Paul, MN: Redleaf Press.

Muldoon, K., Towse, J., Simms, V., Perra, O., & Menzies, V. (2013). A longitudinal analysis of estimation, counting skills, and mathematical ability across the first school year. *Developmental Psychology, 49*(2), 250–257.

Mullis, I.V.S., Martin, M.O., & Foy, P. (2008). *TIMSS 2007 international mathematics report: Findings from IEA's trends international mathematics and science study at the fourth and eighth grades.* Chestnut Hill, MA: Trends in International Mathematics and Science Study (TIMSS) & Progress in International Reading Literacy Study (PIRLS) International Study Center, Lynch School of Education, Boston College.

Naigles, L. (2002). Form is easy, meaning is hard: Resolving a paradox in early child language. *Cognition, 86*(1), 157–199.

Naigles, L., & Hoff-Ginsberg, E. (1995). Input to verb learning: Evidence for the plausibility of syntactic bootstrapping. *Developmental Psychology, 31*(5), 827–837.

National Association for the Education of Young Children (NAEYC). (2009). *Position statement: Developmentally appropriate practice in early childhood programs serving children from birth through to age 8.* Washington, DC: Author.

National Association for the Education of Young Children (NAEYC) & National Council of Teachers of Mathematics (NCTM). (2002). *Early childhood mathematics: Promoting good beginnings. Joint position statement.* Washington, DC: National Association for the Education of Young Children (NAEYC).

National Center for Education Research. (2008). *Effects of preschool curriculum programs on school readiness: Report from the preschool curriculum evaluation research initiative.* Washington, DC: U.S. Department of Education.

National Center for Education Statistics. (2005). *Child care and early education arrangements of infants, toddlers, and preschoolers: 2001.* Washington, DC: U.S. Department of Education, Institute of Education Sciences.

National Center for Education Statistics. (2006). *Teacher qualifications, instructional practices, and reading and mathematics gains of kindergartners.* Washington, DC: U.S. Department of Education.

National Center for Education Statistics. (2013). Program for International Student Assessment (PISA): Mathematics literacy performance of 15-year-olds. Washington, DC: U.S. Department of Education. Retrieved from http://nces.ed.gov/surveys/pisa/pisa2009highlights_3.asp

National Council for Curriculum and Assessment. (2009). *Aistear: The early childhood curriculum framework.* Dublin, Ireland: Government of Ireland.

National Council of Teachers of Mathematics (NCTM). (2000). *Principles and standards for school mathematics.* Reston, VA: Author.

National Research Council. (2005). *Mathematical and scientific development in early childhood: A workshop summary.* Washington, DC: National Academies Press.

Newcombe, N.S., & Frick, A. (2010). Early education for spatial intelligence: Why, what, and how. *Mind, Brain, and Education, 4*(3), 102–111.

Newman, R.S., & Berger, C.F. (1984). Children's numerical estimation: Flexibility in the use of counting. *Journal of Educational Psychology, 76*(1), 55–64.

Noël, M.P. (2005). Finger gnosia: A predictor of numerical abilities in children? *Child Neuropsychology 11*(5), 413–430.

Noël, M.P., Rousselle, L., & Christophe, M. (2005). Magnitude representation in children. In J.I.D. Campbell (Ed.), *Handbook of mathematical cognition* (pp. 179–196). New York, NY: Taylor & Francis.

Nosek, B.A., Smyth, F.L., Sriram, N., Lindner, N.M., Devos, T., Ayala, A., . . . Bergh, R. (2009). National differences in gender-science stereotypes predict national sex differences in science and math achievement. *Proceedings of the National Academy of Sciences, 106*(26), 10593–10597.

Nosworthy, N. (2013). *An investigation of the association between arithmetic achievement and symbolic and nonsymbolic magnitude processing in 5–9 year-old children: Evidence from a paper-and-pencil test* (Doctoral dissertation). Western University, London, Ontario.

O'Bryan, M., Fishbein, H.D., & Ritchey, N. (2004). Intergenerational transmission of prejudice, sex role stereotyping, and intolerance. *Adolescence, 39*(155), 407–426.

Organisation for Economic Co-operation and Development. (2012). *The Programme for International Student Assessment (PISA).* Paris, France: Author. Retrieved from http://www.pisa.oecd.org

Örnkloo, H., & von Hofsten, C. (2007). Fitting objects into holes: On the development of spatial cognition skills. *Developmental Psychology, 43*(2), 404–416.

Outhred, L.N., & Mitchelmore, M.C. (2000). Young children's intuitive understanding of rectangular area measurement. *Journal for Research in Mathematics Education, 31*(2), 144–167.

Pappas, S., Ginsburg, H.P., & Jiang, M. (2003). SES differences in young children's metacognition in the context of mathematical problem solving. *Cognitive Development, 18*(3), 431–450.

Park, B., Chae, J.-L., & Foulks Boyd, B. (2008). Young children's block play and mathematical learning. *Journal of Research in Childhood Education, 23*(2), 157–162.

Patall, E.A., Cooper, H., & Robinson, J.C. (2008). Parent involvement in homework: A research synthesis. *Review of Educational Research, 78*(4), 1039–1101.

Patel, P., & Canobi, K.H. (2010). The role of number words in preschoolers' addition concepts and problem-solving procedures. *Educational Psychology, 30*(2), 107–124.

Patro, K., & Haman, M. (2012). The spatial numerical congruity effect in preschoolers. *Journal of Experimental Child Psychology, 111*(3), 534–542.

Penner-Wilger, M., Fast, L., LeFevre, J.-A., Smith-Chant, B.L., Skwarchuk, S.-L., Kamawar, D., & Bisanz, J. (2007). *The foundations of numeracy: Subitizing, finger gnosia, and fine motor ability.* Paper presented at the 30th annual meeting of the Cognitive Science Society, Austin, TX.

Penner-Wilger, M., Fast, L., LeFevre, J.-A., Smith-Chant, B., Skwarchuk, S.-L., Kamawar, D., & Bisanz, J. (2009). *Subitizing, finger gnosis, and the representation of number.* Paper presented at the 31st annual meeting of the Cognitive Science Society, Amsterdam, the Netherlands.

Pesenti, M., Thioux, M., Seron, X., & De Volder, A. (2000). Neuroanatomical substrate of Arabic number processing, numerical comparison and simple addition: A PET study. *Journal of Cognitive Neuroscience, 121*(3), 461–479.

Pezdek, K., Berry, T., & Renno, P.A. (2002). Children's mathematics achievement: The role of parents' perceptions and their involvement in homework. *Journal of Educational Psychology, 94*(4), 771.

Piaget, J. (1962). *Play, dreams and imitation.* New York, NY: Norton.

Piaget, J. (1976/Original work published 1929). *The child's conception of the world.* Savage, MD: Littlefield Adams.

Piaget, J., & Inhelder, B. (1969). *The psychology of the child.* New York, NY: Basic Books.

Piaget, J., Inhelder, B., & Szeminska, A. (1960). *The child's conception of geometry.* London: Routledge and Kegan Paul.

Pianta, R.C., Barnett, W.S., Burchinal, M., & Thornburg, K.R. (2009). The effects of preschool education: What we know, how public policy is or is not aligned with the evidence base, and what we need to know. *Psychological Science in the Public Interest, 10*(2), 49–88.

Piccolo, D.L., & Test, J. (2011). Preschoolers' thinking during block play. *Teaching Children Mathematics, 17*(5), 310–316.

Powel, W.D., Morelli, T., & Nusbaum, N. (1994). Performance and confidence estimates in preschool and young grade-school children. *Child Study Journal, 24*(1), 23–47.

Pramling, I. (1983). *The child's conception of learning.* Gothenburg, Sweden: Acta Universitatis Gothoburgensis.

Pramling Samuelsson, I., & Asplund Carlsson, M. (2008). The playing learning child: Towards a pedagogy of early childhood. *Scandinavian Journal of Educational Research, 52*(6), 623–641.

Pramling Samuelsson, I., & Johansson, E. (2009). Why do children involve teachers in their play and learning? *European Early Childhood Education Research Journal, 17*(1), 77–94.

Programme for International Student Assessment (PISA). (2006). Learning for tomorrow's world—First results from PISA 2003. Retrieved from http://www.pisa.oecd.org/dataoecd/58/41/33917867.pdf

Pruden, S.M., Levine, S.C., & Huttenlocher, J. (2011). Children's spatial thinking: Does talk about the spatial world matter? *Developmental Science, 14*(6), 1417–1430.

Rasmussen, C., & Bisanz, J. (2005). Representation and working memory in early arithmetic. *Journal of Experimental Child Psychology, 91*(2), 137–157.

Reynolds, F.J., & Reeve, R.A. (2001). Gesture in collaborative mathematics problem-solving. *Journal of Mathematical Behavior, 20*(4), 447–460.

Rideout, V. (2011). *Zero to eight: Children's media use in America.* San Francisco, CA: Common Sense Media.

Robinson, J.P. (2010). The effects of test translation on young English learners' mathematical performance. *Educational Researcher, 39*(8), 582–590.

Rochat, P., & Hespos, S.J. (1996). Tracking and anticipation of invisible spatial transformations by 4- to 8-month-old infants. *Cognitive Development, 11*(1), 3–17.

Romano, E., Babchishin, L., Pagani, L.S., & Kohen, D. (2010). School readiness and later achievement: Replication and extension using a nationwide Canadian survey. *Developmental Psychology, 46*(5), 995–1007.

Ruff, H.A., & Lawson, K.R. (1990). Development of sustained, focused attention in young children during free play. *Developmental Psychology, 26*(1), 85–93.

Sarama, J., & Clements, D.H. (2009). *Early childhood mathematics education research: Learning trajectories for young children.* New York, NY: Routledge.

Sarnecka, B.W., & Carey, S. (2008). How counting represents number: What children must learn and when they learn it. *Cognition, 108*(3), 662–674.

Sasanguie, D., De Smedt, B., Defever, E., & Reynvoet, B. (2012). Association between basic numerical abilities and mathematics achievement. *British Journal of Developmental Psychology, 30*(2), 344–357.

Saxe, G.B., & Kaplan, R. (1981). Gesture in early counting: A developmental analysis. *Perceptual and Motor Skills, 53*(3), 851–854.

Schmidt, W.H., Tatto, M.T., Bankov, K., Blömeke, S., Cedillo, T., Cogan, L., . . . Schwille, J. (2007). *The preparation gap: Teacher education for middle school mathematics in six countries.* Lansing, MI: MSE Center for Research in Mathematics Education.

Seo, K.-H., & Ginsburg, H. (2004). What is developmentally appropriate in early childhood mathematics education? Lessons from new research. In D.H. Clements, J. Sarama, & A.-M. DiBiase (Eds.), *Engaging young children in mathematics: Standards for early childhood mathematics education* (pp. 91–104). Mahwah, NJ: Lawrence Erlbaum Associates.

Sfard, A. (2009). What's all the fuss about gestures? A commentary. *Educational Studies in Mathematics, 70*(2), 191–200.

Shiakalli, M.A., & Zacharos, K. (2012). The contribution of external representations in pre-school mathematical problem solving. *International Journal of Early Years Education, 20*(4), 315–331.

Shonkoff, J.P. (2009). Investment in early childhood development lays the foundation for a prosperous and sustainable society. In R.E. Tremblay, R.G. Barr, R.D.V. Peters, & M. Boivin (Eds.), *Encyclopedia on early childhood development* (pp. 1–5). Montreal, Quebec: Centre of Excellence for Early Childhood Development.

Siegler, R.S., & Booth, J.L. (2005). Development of numerical estimation. In J.I.D. Campbell (Ed.), *Handbook of mathematical cognition* (pp. 197–212). New York, NY: Taylor & Francis.

Siegler, R.S., & Jenkins, E. (1989). *How children discover new strategies.* Hillsdale, NJ: Lawrence Erlbaum Associates.

Siegler, R.S., & Opfer, J. (2003). The development of numerical estimation: Evidence of multiple representations of numerical quantity. *Psychological Science, 14*(3), 237–243.

Siegler, R.S., & Robinson, M. (1982). The development of numerical understandings. In H.W. Reese & L.P. Lipsett (Eds.), *Advances in child development and behavior* (Vol. 16, pp. 242–312). New York, NY: Academic Press.

Simplicio, J.S.C. (2005). Homework in the 21st century: The antiquated and ineffectual implementation of a time honored educational strategy. *Education, 126*(1), 138–142.

Singer-Freeman, K.E., & Goswami, U. (2001). Does half a pizza equal half a box of chocolates? Proportional matching in an analogy task. *Cognitive Development, 16*(3), 811–829.

Siraj-Blatchford, I., & Manni, L. (2008). "Would you like to tidy up now?" An analysis of adult questioning in the English Foundation Stage. *Early Years 28*(1), 5–22.

Siraj-Blatchford, I., Sylva, K., Muttoch, S., Gilden, R., & Bell, D. (2002). *Researching effective pedagogy in the early years.* Oxford: University of Oxford, Department of Educational Studies.

Skwarchuk, S.-L. (2009). How do parents support preschoolers' numeracy learning experiences at home? *Early Childhood Education Journal, 37*(3), 189–197.

Sleeter, C.E. (2011). An agenda to strengthen culturally responsive pedagogy. *English Teaching: Practice & Critique, 10*(2), 7–23.

Smith, L.B. (2009). From fragments to geometric shape: Changes in visual object recognition between 18 and 24 months. *Current Directions in Psychological Science, 18*(5), 290–294.

Sophian, C. (1988). Limitations on preschool children's knowledge about counting: Using counting to compare to two sets. *Developmental Psychology, 24*(5), 634–640.

Sophian, C., & Wood, A. (1997). Proportional reasoning in young children: The parts and the whole of it. *Journal of Educational Psychology, 89*(2), 309–317.

Spelke, E.S. (1994). Preferential looking and intermodal perception in infancy: Comment on Lewkowicz (1992). *Infant Behaviour and Development, 17*(3), 285–287.

Spinillo, A.G., & Bryant, P. (1991). Children's proportional judgments: The importance of "half." *Child Development, 62*(3), 427–440.

Spinillo, A.G., & Bryant, P. (1999). Proportional reasoning in young children: Part-part comparisons about continuous and discontinuous quantity. *Mathematical Cognition, 5*(2), 181–197.

Starkey, P. (1992). The early development of numerical reasoning. *Cognition, 43*(2), 93–126.

Starkey, P., & Cooper, R. (1980). Perception of numbers by human infants. *Science, 210*(4473), 1033–1035.

Starkey, P., & Gelman, R. (1982). The development of addition and subtraction abilities prior to formal schooling in arithmetic. In T.P. Carpenter, J.M. Moser, & T.A. Romberg (Eds.), *Addition and subtraction: A cognitive perspective* (pp. 99–116). Hillsdale, NJ: Erlbaum.

Starkey, P., Spelke, E., & Gelman, R. (1983). Detection of intermodal numerical correspondences by human infants. *Science, 222*(4620), 179–181.

Starkey, P., Spelke, E., & Gelman, R. (1990). Numerical abstraction by human infants. *Cognition, 36*(2), 97–128.

Statistics Canada. (2005). *The adult literacy and life skills survey.* Ottawa, Canada: Government of Canada. Retrieved from http://www5.statcan.gc.ca/bsolc/olc-cel/olc-cel?catno=89-603-XWE&lang=eng

Steele, J. (2003). Children's gender stereotypes about math: The role of gender stratification. *Journal of Applied Social Psychology, 33*(12), 2587–2606.

Stipek, D.J., & Gralinski, J.H. (1991). Gender differences in children's achievement related beliefs and emotional responses to success and failure in mathematics. *Journal of Educational Psychology, 83*(3), 361–371.

Stylianides, G.J., & Stylianides, A.J. (2009). Mathematics for teaching: A form of applied mathematics. *Teaching and Teacher Education, 26*(2), 161–172.

Sutton-Smith, B. (1997). *The ambiguity of play.* Cambridge, MA: Harvard University Press.

Szilágyi, J., Clements, D.H., & Sarama, J. (2013). Young children's understandings of length measurement: Evaluating a learning trajectory. *Journal for Research in Mathematics Education, 44*(3), 581–620.

Tam, V.C., & Chan, R.M. (2009). Parental involvement in primary children's homework in Hong Kong. *School Community Journal, 19*(2), 81–100.

Tardif, T., Shatz, M., & Naigles, L. (1997). Caregiver speech and children's use of nouns versus verbs: A comparison of English, Italian, and Mandarin. *Journal of Child Language, 24*(3), 535–565.

Tarim, K. (2009). The effects of cooperative learning on preschoolers' mathematics problem-solving ability. *Educational Studies in Mathematics, 72*(3), 325–340.

Torres-Velasquez, D., & Lobo, G. (2004). Culturally responsive mathematics teaching and English language learners. *Teaching Children Mathematics, 11*(5), 249–255.

Tudge, J., & Doucet, F. (2004). Early mathematics experiences: Observing young black and white children's everyday activities. *Early Childhood Research Quarterly, 19*(1), 21–39.

Twomey Fosnot, C., & Dolk, M. (2001). *Young mathematicians at work: Constructing fractions, decimals, and percent.* Portsmouth, NH: Heinemann.

Uren, N.S.K. (2008). Pretend play, social competence and involvement in children aged 5–7 years: The concurrent validity of the child-initiated pretend play assessment. *Australian Occupational Therapy Journal, 56*(1), 33–40.

Uttal, D.H., Meadow, N.G., Tipton, E., Hand, L.L., Alden, A.R., Warren, C., & Newcombe, N.S. (2013). The malleability of spatial skills: A meta-analysis of training studies. *Psychological Bulletin, 139*(2), 352–402.

VanDerHeyden, A.M., Broussard, C., & Cooley, A. (2006). Further development of measures of early math performance for preschoolers. *Journal of School Psychology, 44*(6), 533–553.

van Oers, B. (1996). Are you sure? Stimulating mathematical thinking during young children's play. *European Early Childhood Education Research Journal, 4*(1), 71–87.

van Oers, B. (2010). Emergent mathematical thinking in the context of play. *Educational Studies in Mathematics, 74*(1), 23–37.

Vine, K.W. (1985). Development of linear measurement in five- and six-year-old children. *Genetic, Social, and General Psychology Monographs, 111*(4), 455–503.

Vygotsky, L.S. (1962). *Thought and language.* Cambridge, MA: MIT Press.

Vygotsky, L.S. (1978). *Mind in society.* Cambridge, MA: Harvard University Press.

Wagner, S.W., & Walters, J. (1982). A longitudinal analysis of early number concepts: From numbers to number. In G.E. Forman (Ed.), *Action and thought* (pp. 137–161). New York, NY: Academic Press.

Welsh, M.C., Friedman, S.L., & Spieker, S.J. (2006). Executive functions in developing children: Current conceptualizations and questions for the future. In K. McCartney & D. Phillips (Eds.), *The Blackwell handbook of early childhood development* (pp. 167–187). Malden, MA: Blackwell Publishing.

Whitebread, D. (2010). Play, metacognition and self-regulation. In P. Broadhead, J. Howard, & E. Wood (Eds.), *Play and learning in the early years* (pp. 161–176). Thousand Oaks, CA: Sage Publications.

Winton, P., & Buysse, V. (Eds.). (2005). *Early developments* (Vol. 9). Chapel Hill, NC: Frank Porter Graham Child Development Institute, University of North Carolina at Chapel Hill.

Wood, E. (2010). Developing and integrated pedagogical approaches to play and learning. In P. Broadhead, J. Howard, & E. Wood (Eds.), *Play and learning in the early years* (pp. 9–26). Thousand Oaks, CA: Sage Publications.

Wynn, K. (1990). Children's understanding of counting. *Cognition, 36*(2), 155–193.

Wynn, K. (1992a). Addition and subtraction by human infants. *Nature, 358*(6389), 749–750.

Wynn, K. (1992b). Children's acquisition of the number words and the counting system. *Cognitive Psychology, 24*(2), 240–251.

Xu, F., & Spelke, E. (2000). Large number discrimination in 6-month-old infants. *Cognition, 74*(1), B1–B11.

Yackel, E. (1997). A foundation for algebraic reasoning in the early grades. *Teaching Children Mathematics, 3*(6), 276–280.

Zero to Three. (2009). *Brain development.* Washington, DC: National Center for Infants, Toddlers, and Families. Retrieved from http://www.zerotothree.org/child-development/brain-development

Zorzi, M., Priftis, K., & Umiltà, C. (2002). Neglect disrupts the mental number line. *Nature, 417*(6885), 138–139.

Index

Figures are indicated by the letter *f*.